Life can feel overwhelming, bi
on finding peace and the joy
swept up in the world's chaos. Through relatable
dation in Scripture, Samantha Decker provides a timely and heartfelt
guide to creating margin and surrendering control. Her encouraging
words resonate deeply, pointing us toward the transformative rest and
freedom found in trusting Jesus.

AMY CORDOVA
Oklahoma Baptist Missions and Women's Ministry Partner

In our fast-paced world, Samantha will remind you of what really matters through study and reflection on God's commands to rest, trust, and
surrender. She has a way of drawing you in with depth and practicality.
This book is a must-read for anyone who is trying to do it all!

LAUREN VANDER LINDEN
Speaker and author of *I Want to Move On*

How often do we dream of unhurried days? Even when we do, living a life
of rest is not taking a nap, but living a life of abiding in Christ. Samantha
helps her readers understand their calendar and to-do list might be full,
but creating margin to spend time with Christ is not only a good thing
but a necessary thing. Reading *Unhurried* will help you learn new priorities, but it will mostly draw you closer to the One who gives life and
gives it abundantly.

DR. KELLY D. KING
Women's Minister, Quail Springs Baptist Church, Oklahoma City;
Visiting Professor of Christian Ministry, Southeastern Baptist
Theological Seminary

It has become normal, even celebrated, for individuals and families to run
through life at an unsustainable pace. Overscheduled and overcommitted
has become normal language in our society, and we wear it as a badge of
honor. Samantha reminds us of God's original design and encourages
us to live with eternity in mind. All throughout her book, you see the
constant reminder of the importance of slowing down, creating margin,
and practicing rest. She supports these reminders with biblical examples
and personal experiences. After reading this book, you will have the tools
in your toolbox to reorient your life, say "no," and live an unhurried life.

DR. JEFF DEGIACOMO
Senior Pastor, Immanuel Baptist Church Shawnee

Samantha offers practical steps to realign our busy lives with eternal priorities. This message couldn't be more timely or needed in today's fast-paced world.

JULIE BUSLER
Author, speaker, and Bible teacher

We have known Samantha for years. We were literally her neighbors; I was also her pastor. My wife, Julie, led her small group. She is the real deal; an authentic, honest, committed disciple of Jesus. We are excited that you now have an opportunity to know her heart through this book. In *Unhurried*, Samantha challenges us to develop a different way of life that "starts with opening your schedule and asking God to guide your steps." Who wouldn't benefit from a life with that kind of margin?

JULIE DILBECK
DR. HANCE DILBECK
President of GuideStone Financial Resources

In *Unhurried*, Samantha Decker is kind to our souls. She gently exposes our busy, over-scheduled lives (including her own) and calls us to a better, slower way of living. She helps us hear God asking us to trust His good plans and let go of our white-knuckle grip on life. Her honest stories, biblical examples, thoughtful questions, and practical advice all move our hearts to want the very thing we know we need: margin and rest.

NATALIE ABBOTT
Author, Bible teacher, and cofounder of Dwell Differently

Samantha Decker writes with the same spirit of warmth and welcome that marks her life. A book about rest needs such an author, who comes alongside her reader as a fellow companion on this hurried journey of life and says, "Me too, friend. Here's how God helped me." Providing spiritual insights, timeless wisdom, and practical helps, *Unhurried* addresses both the discipline and delight of the essential human need and biblical expectation of rest. No guilt trips here, but an invitation to discover how *less* leads to *more*—more quality time, more energy, and ultimately more of the best version of you.

DR. COURTNEY J. VEASEY
Teaching Fellow in Biblical Studies and Biblical Languages for the Alexandrian Institute for Scripture and Theology

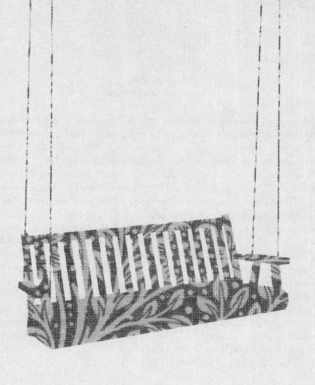

UNHURRIED

An Invitation to Slow Down, Create Margin,
and Surrender Control to God

SAMANTHA DECKER

MOODY PUBLISHERS
CHICAGO

Edited by Pamela Joy Pugh
Interior design: Brandi Davis
Cover design: Good Mood Design Co / Riley Moody
Cover image pattern of woven cotton, courtesy of clevelandart/Unsplash.

ISBN: 978-0-8024-3327-5

Originally delivered by fleets of horse-drawn wagons, the affordable paperbacks from D. L. Moody's publishing house resourced the church and served everyday people. Now, after more than 125 years of publishing and ministry, Moody Publishers' mission remains the same—even if our delivery systems have changed a bit. For more information on other books (and resources) created from a biblical perspective, go to www.moodypublishers.com or write to:

Moody Publishers
820 N. LaSalle Boulevard
Chicago, IL 60610

1 3 5 7 9 10 8 6 4 2

Printed in Colombia

To my husband, Dustin,
and our children, Eli, Caden, Hudson, and Charlie.

God called me to slow down, and in many ways,
He used you to show me how.
Thank you for making me more like Jesus.
I love you . . . so much!

CONTENTS

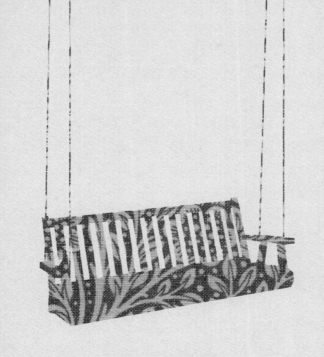

PART ONE

THE PROBLEM OF HURRY, CONTROL, AND AN OVER-PLANNED LIFE

CHAPTER ONE

IN THE CHAOS

Now this is what the LORD Almighty says: "Give careful
thought to your ways. You have planted much, but harvested
little. You eat, but never have enough. You drink, but never
have your fill. You put on clothes, but are not warm. You
earn wages, only to put them in a purse with holes in it."

HAGGAI 1:5–6 (NIV)

With tired eyes, sagging shoulders, and an aching lower back, I placed the computer on top of my seven-month pregnant belly and opened it. However, as soon as I started digging through the pile of unending work emails, my two-year-old screamed my name from the bathroom—which is never a good thing—the doorbell rang, and the oven timer beeped.

Rushed, I ran to get the one-sheet-pan dinner out of the oven, motioned to my friend to come on in and drop off the sippy cup my son had left at her house the day before, and dashed to inspect the damage done to the bathroom (let's just say toilet paper was everywhere).

Not only that, but as I looked around, I saw every toy tractor, truck, and train we owned lined up along our cherry-walnut chest my Papa made me, loads of laundry overflowing, mail piled up on the counter, and a general state of mess. I was swimming in chaos.

Busy was the norm, and because it had become my norm, I wasn't stressed or overwhelmed. And yet, I wasn't present.

I had made my life hurried.

I spent most of my days jumping from one task to the next. I had become a master at marking off my to-do list, multitasking, and making plans obsessively.

As pastor and author Ben Stuart describes it in his book *Rest & War*, I felt like an octopus on roller skates[1]—plenty of movement, just not necessarily forward; busy, but not productive.

That same fall evening, I walked down the worn pathway to the mailbox and my kind neighbor casually asked how things were going. I responded as I normally did: "Oh, I'm good, busy . . . but good." Her response is what stuck with me. She said, "I don't know how you do it all."

Honestly, at that moment, her words felt like a badge of honor. They meant I was doing more than she was, that she was impressed with how much I could do, and in some way, I was achieving more. My ugly, selfish pride surged.

Later, I opened my Bible, planning to do my daily Bible reading I hadn't seemed to have time for earlier in the day. I opened to Haggai only to read this:

> Now this is what the LORD Almighty says: "Give careful thought to your ways. You have planted much, but harvested little. You eat, but never have enough. You drink, but never have your fill. You put on clothes, but are not warm. You earn wages, only to put them in a purse with holes in it."
> Haggai 1:5–6 (NIV)

In the stillness of the night, the Lord's conviction came raining down as my sweet neighbor's words echoed in my mind.

"I don't know how you do it all."

Those few words weren't a badge of honor; they were a call to action. They were an indication my life was full of misplaced priorities. Like the people Haggai addressed, I was striving, but never satisfied. I was failing to do what God had called me to do and be who God had called me to be. My life was like "a purse with holes in it."[2]

In the book of Haggai, the temple was destroyed, and yet God's people focused on building their own houses and pursuing their own success instead of following the Lord's command to rebuild His temple. So often, we are like these Israelites. We pursue financial security, job success, do-it-all parenting, and endless pleasures over the commands and will of God.

This book is about slowing down, creating space, and ultimately joining God in the work He is already doing.

What about you? Are you exhausted from planning and re-planning, and still feeling like you can't get it all done? Does it seem like you're constantly on the go, physically or mentally, and rest is unattainable? Have you traded peace, ease, and purpose for striving, achieving, and success?

The good news is God will meet us where we are and work within our schedules and circumstances if we let Him. This may involve replacing "good" things with the things God's calling us to do or looking for opportunities to say a sacred no when our plates are full.

However, the reality of "doing it all" and "being busy" is probably present in your life as well. We are encouraged and often even forced to be on the go. We say yes without thinking. We make plans to have plans and fail to set and maintain the boundaries we desperately need.

As a result of this hurried and busy lifestyle, we sacrifice what we don't even realize we are sacrificing: the things that matter.

An article in the *New York Post* reported that American families get just 37 minutes of quality time together per day.[3] Thirty-seven minutes. There are 1,440 minutes in a day. Our quality time comprises just a little over 2.5 percent. What are we doing with the other 97.5 percent?

Once the reality of this lifestyle began to soak in, I started asking God to show me what I was missing.

What did Scripture show me? What did the people far wiser and more experienced than me do to prevent this chaos? How could I slow down, eliminate the mess, and make time for the things that matter? The most basic answer I discovered was the need to lay aside my plans for the purposes of God. I needed to create margin.

This book is about slowing down, creating space, and ultimately joining God in the work He is already doing. It's a call to make small, moment-by-moment changes that have the potential to impact eternity. Above all, this book is written to give God glory: glory in my words and in my actions, and in the bigger story they tell.

This is the story of a God who knows how to rest. A God who has everything under control. A God who gave His only Son to save us from our sins and the bondage they bring. In Christ, there is freedom from striving, busyness, and hurry. But it requires surrender. Are you ready to take off these weights and follow Jesus with every area of your life?

The first three chapters of this book identify and break down the problem of hurry and control. When we pry our fingers off the objects we hold the tightest, we make room for God to heal, teach, and replace our idols with the things of God. Chapters 4 through 10 focus on the processes and tools we need to slow down. These chapters apply the truths found in God's Word as the remedy for this epidemic of hurry. Finally, chapters 11 through 14 offer tried practices and applications for those who are committed to making a change. As we hunger for the purposes of God and take active steps toward inviting Him to direct our paths, we'll find that our pace will slow and our eyes will open. Soon our perspective will change.

In Christ, you have everything you need to slow down.

Recently I stood in front of a traditional church pew and sang the old hymn "Be Thou My Vision." As I sang (not well, I may add), tears streamed down my face as the words became a prayer, a plea, and a confession of my inadequacy and Jesus' sufficiency. I knew in order to change my perspective, I needed Jesus to become my vision. Everything must filter through the lens of Christ: what I see and plan, even what I think.

Tradition tells us an Irish monk named Dallán Forgaill wrote this as a poem in the sixth century as he reflected on the faithfulness of St. Patrick, a missionary to Ireland in the fifth century. Many years later, in the early 1900s, Eleanor Hull versified the text into a hymn. The first verse of the hymn is this:

> Be Thou my vision, O Lord of my heart;
> naught be all else to me, save that Thou art.
> Thou my best thought, by day or by night,
> waking or sleeping, Thy presence my light.

For generations, followers of Jesus have recognized our deep need to see as Jesus sees and think as Jesus thinks. Forgaill, Hull, and countless other believers have pleaded with the Lord to guide their steps and light their path. The song ends in this way:

> High King of heaven, my victory won,
> may I reach heaven's joys, O bright heav'n's Sun!

Heart of my own heart, whatever befall,

still be my vision, O Ruler of all.[4]

Don't miss this. The victory is won! We serve and follow the High King, the Ruler of all. He was sufficient for the generations of believers who prayed this before you, and still is sufficient for you and me too.

So, before we get in too deep, know this: in Christ, you have everything you need to slow down. You have everything you need to rest and relinquish control and spend time with your King. Dive in, ask the Lord to be your vision, and trust in His sufficiency.

My prayer is this book challenges your pace, your priorities, and your plans, and shows you a God who wants you to abide with Him.

At the end of each chapter, you'll find a few questions for reflection and a verse to memorize. These questions are designed to help you pause and ask the Lord what it is He wants you to learn and apply to your life. This can be done individually or in community. The verse is intended to help you hide God's Word in your heart so you can better apply what you've learned. And if, like me, your tendency is to skip right over these and rush to the next thing (sound familiar?), my challenge to you is to use these questions and this verse to force yourself to slow down. You might be surprised at what God has for you!

QUESTIONS FOR REFLECTION

1. *Have you ever described your life as "busy"? What are some things that make it feel this way?*

2. *Does busyness feel like a good thing to you? Why or why not?*

3. *How does a hurried life affect your view of God?*

VERSE TO MEMORIZE

Now this is what the LORD Almighty says:
"Give careful thought to your ways."

—HAGGAI 1:5 (NIV)

CHAPTER TWO

WHAT IS MARGIN?

And rising very early in the morning, while it was still dark,
he departed and went out to a desolate place,
and there he prayed.

MARK 1:35

My Memaw is the epitome of an English teacher. She taught English for thirty-five years in a small public school in Crane, Texas. Unofficially, she also taught each of her seven grandchildren and still takes opportunities to teach her fourteen (and counting) great-grandchildren, too.

I have vivid memories of riding in the backseat of my grandparents' blue Mercury with my sister, enjoying our "assignments." Memaw would hand us a well-read page of the newspaper and encourage (or force . . . you choose) us to circle the verbs, identify metaphors, find typos, and define words. Looking back, her love of learning and writing is what led me to enjoy writing. To this day, I enjoy defining words. I love to see deeper meanings and practical applications. Before I lose any of you who tune out the minute a part of speech is mentioned, I want to put the definition of a specific word before you: margin.

INTENTIONAL MARGINS

Margin is defined as:[5]

1. the part of a page or sheet outside the main body of printed or written matter
2. a spare amount or measure or degree allowed or given for contingencies or special situations

The first definition captures the literal margin around a physical sheet of paper. As I think through this definition, I think of space for notes, afterthoughts, and words or pictures designed to be outside the lines. My sister is an incredibly gifted professional artist, and her doodles are always much more impressive than my starbursts and swirls. However, the quality isn't necessarily what matters; it is the space to create and reflect that I love.

But it's the second definition I needed in my life. Pause with me after "a spare amount." When was the last time you felt like you had a spare amount of time? Time left over after work, chores, play, or even quality time with a friend. Time that was just extra. If you're having difficulty identifying space in your schedule, chances are you need margin in your life.

If you keep reading the second definition, you'll notice margin is given (or created) for contingencies or special situations. I believe a better way of defining "contingencies or special situations" is "God moments." God works in our schedules and works in the normalcy of a day, but He is so much bigger. He works in special situations too, in the space much larger than your plans. The catch? You have to choose to create room.

Scripture is full of examples and insight into this process of creating margin.

Jesus Created Margin

Mark 1 documents the start of Jesus' earthly ministry. He called the disciples, healed the sick and demon-possessed, and even healed Simon's mother-in-law in her home. His ministry started to gain attention to the extent that verse 33 says, "And the whole city was gathered together at the door."

Take a minute to pause here. I'm not sure how many people lived in this city, but even in the smallest city, if everyone gathered at your door, I think you'd feel a little overwhelmed. You may think this sounds like the opposite of creating margin, but that's because we haven't read what's coming.

In verse 35, Scripture says, "And rising very early in the morning, while it was still dark, he departed and went out to a desolate place, and there he prayed." This sounds a lot like "a spare amount of time given for special situations." Jesus created margin. He knew how important it was to get away from the chaos, be alone, and talk to the Father.

Mark made a point to let us know it was still dark outside. He doesn't tell us the exact time, but we know it was before the sun came up. Jesus was fully God, but also fully human. This means He experienced tiredness and fatigue just as we do. Now, even if He was a morning person, getting up and going out before the sun was even up was a choice. It was deliberate and intentional. He had to choose to create margin.

If Jesus created margin, shouldn't we? Maybe this requires getting up while it's still dark outside. Maybe it's using your toddler's naptime to pray in the quiet instead of cleaning the house. Maybe you should use your lunch break as an opportunity to spend time in the Word. Where is there space to create margin in your schedule?

Jesus wasn't the only one who created margin.

Philip's Example of Living Unhurried

In Acts 6:1–7, we read that the followers of Jesus increased in number, and the disciples tried to do it all. But couldn't. Not the point of the story, but if I were guessing, they probably weren't working to create much margin. As a solution, they chose seven men to serve, one of whom was Philip.

The next time we see Philip is in Acts 8:4–8, in the city of Samaria proclaiming Christ and performing signs. Scripture tells us there was "much joy in that city." From an outward, worldly perspective, Philip had no reason to leave where he was or stop doing what he was doing. People were paying attention to what he was saying, and his ministry was excelling. However, God had something else planned.

Acts 8:26–27a says this: "Now an angel of the Lord said to Philip, 'Rise and go toward the south to the road that goes down from Jerusalem to Gaza.' This is a desert place. And he rose and went."

"He rose and went." He didn't stop and explain to God that walking to the desert wasn't on his to-do list. He didn't ask God for more specifics or details before he decided if he would go or not. He simply "rose and went." Philip's desire for obedience was more important to him than his to-do list, his plans for the day, and even his thriving ministry in Samaria. He had made room in his life for special situations like these.

> I wonder how many times we miss opportunities because we are too hurried and too focused on getting back to where we think we should be.

Continuing on in Acts 8, you learn the Spirit led Philip to an Ethiopian eunuch who was reading the book of Isaiah yet struggling to understand. Philip, starting with the passage the Ethiopian was reading, shared the good news of Jesus. Immediately after, Philip baptized his new brother in the faith.

Take a minute to think about this: Because Philip was obedient and committed to following the Spirit over his own plans, a man gained eternal life. Not only that, but this man carried the gospel back with him to Ethiopia, furthering the gospel movement. There's no way we could know the full impact of this encounter!

The story concludes in verses 39–40.

> And when they came up out of the water, the Spirit of the Lord carried Philip away, and the eunuch saw him no more, and went on his way rejoicing. But Philip found himself at Azotus, and as he passed through he preached the gospel to all the towns until he came to Caesarea.

I love this! Philip could've easily told the Lord, "Okay God, I'll go, but I'm heading straight to Samaria to jump back into my ministry. It's comfortable, it's successful, and I need to get back to keep the momentum going. I have responsibilities!" However, Philip responded differently. The Spirit carried him away to Azotus (I'd love to know more what this was like!). Then, "as he passed through," Philip preached the gospel.

Again, Philip isn't rushing back to where he thinks he should be—he's taking steps and asking the Lord for opportunities along the way. Then, when the Lord answers, Philip is obedient.

I wonder how many times we miss opportunities because we are too hurried and too focused on getting back to where we think we should be. The start of obedience often involves pausing and listening to the promptings of the Spirit.

BECOMING A FRONT-PORCH PERSON

Several years ago, I intentionally began seeking the Lord for insight and guidance for the year to come. Little did I know what I was asking at the time . . .

As I prayed, I remember so clearly the Lord simply telling me to "draw near." Desiring more, I read in Leviticus how Moses and Aaron had to draw near to the altar before they could offer the Israelites' sacrifices (Lev. 9:7). I discovered in Hebrews that we are commanded to draw near to the throne of grace to receive mercy and help in our time of need (Heb. 4:16). And I studied in James how when we draw near to God, He draws near to us (James 4:8).

So as I started to "draw near" by digging into the Word and spending time in prayer, I knew God was preparing me for changes ahead.

A few months later, both my best friend and my cousin moved out of state due to job changes or transfers. In the midst of this, my husband and I also felt the Lord opening doors to move away from the neighbors we loved, invested in, and sought community with to a home in another area of our city.

So in a short period of time, my community was now completely different. However, I'm so grateful the Lord told me to draw near because I knew these changes were opportunities for more than just new neighbors. These changes were opportunities to create margin and join God in the work He was already doing in our new neighborhood.

My husband and I began praying for our new neighbors. We also challenged ourselves to meet every person on our street within the first few weeks of moving in. I had my kids help me bake cookies, and we hand-delivered cards with our phone numbers on them, letting each neighbor know we were praying for them.

However, I knew in order to create margin, I needed to do more. I decided to become a "front-porch person." My husband is a gifted woodworker and one of the first projects I asked him to craft was a porch swing. He built a beautiful swing out of pine and hung it for me within the week.

I began setting aside time each day to sit on my swing. As I sat and swayed back and forth, I started praying for neighbors to come out with their kids, or check their mail, or take their trash out. And when they did, I'd make an effort to have a conversation with them.

> **At the peak of my hurry, I believed sitting was pointless and idle. This belief is a lie. God works while we wait.**

My time on the swing became the highlight of my day. Some days, my boys would play happily for an extended period, and other days there would be full-on two-year-old meltdowns right in the front flower bed. But the quantity of time and external circumstances weren't what mattered. God was softening my heart, opening my eyes, and slowing my pace through porch-sitting.

To be honest, there was a time in my life when sitting on a porch swing would have felt like a waste. I would've come up with a list of a hundred other things needing to be done instead. At the peak of my hurry, I believed sitting was pointless and idle. This belief is a lie.

Do you have a hard time just sitting? Are you so caught up in productivity that intentionally slowing for even a few moments feels wasteful? Is your instinct to look at your phone the second you stop moving?

Let me challenge you with this: God works while we wait.

Through sitting on my porch swing and praying for my neighbors, the Lord created opportunities. He provided clear openings to invite neighbors to church and to women's Bible study, to share my testimony, and to have conversations about the gospel.

In the days where everything felt shut down or weird or different, I was able to deepen relationships and meet my neighbors' needs simply by slowing down and looking for God-given opportunities.

When God tells us to love our neighbor, He doesn't *just* mean the people right next door. But it does include the people right next door. In what ways might He be calling you to be a front-porch person too? At work? Your kid's school? Soccer practice? To the cashier at the grocery store or the server at the restaurant? Here's the point: being a front-porch person is less about the location and more about being present and available for the Lord to use you as He wills.

The Creator Rested

This idea of sitting, resting, and creating downtime is not new. In fact, it goes back to the creation narrative in Genesis.

Many of us are familiar with the story of creation in Genesis 1. From our earliest days in Sunday school we've been taught, "In the beginning, God created the heavens and the earth" (Gen. 1:1). Usually, this was coupled with a coloring sheet of the earth and a toddler melody of "He's Got the Whole World in His Hands."

However, the lack of novelty should never diminish the miraculous work God performed.

In the original Hebrew, the word "created" literally means "formed *ex nihilo*—out of nothing."[6] There was nothing, and God used nothing to form everything.

Then, we read this in Genesis 2:1–3:

> Thus the heavens and the earth were finished, and all the host of them. And on the seventh day God finished his work that he had done, and he rested on the seventh day from all his work that he had done. So God blessed the seventh day

and made it holy, because on it God rested from all his work that he had done in creation.

When it comes to creating margin, we see two important practices in these verses.

God Recognized When He Was Finished

He could've kept tweaking His work, or creating more and more because He is God, but He didn't. "God finished His work."

When was the last time you finished your work? I don't necessarily mean completed everything on your to-do list with absolutely nothing left to do, but instead, finished your work for an allotted time.

When we live hurried, over-planned lives, we fail to recognize finished work because there is always more to do.

This is a hard principle for me to put into place. Finishing work when I know there's more to do feels a lot like procrastination. However, in this account, God lovingly shows us a key difference. Procrastination is avoiding work you need to do, whereas finishing is completing the work you set out to do. This doesn't mean you finish more than you set out to do, it means you finish the work and recognize it is enough.

God Rested from His Work

When the work was complete, God rested.

I think this is one of the most powerful and freeing images of God in Scripture. The Creator of the universe prioritized stopping, slowing, and resting. Then He took it even further by blessing this time and making it holy. This idea of "sabbath," or a day or time to abstain from work, becomes a major theme we see throughout Scripture (more on this in chapter 8).

Yet, when we fail to create margin and make time for rest, we essentially tell God we are more important than Him—a dangerous and ill-considered lie. If the Creator of the universe can make time for rest and designate this time as holy, how much more should we find time away from work? There is nothing you need to do that is more important than the work God accomplished.

This realization should bring freedom! You can create margin, you can sit on your metaphorical porch swing, and you can stop working because God rested.

What does rest look like for you?

PRACTICAL PROCESSES
FOR CREATING MARGIN

As you read on, you'll discover this book is not designed to give you time-management tips or act as a "how-to-slow-down" guide. Instead, rooted in the Word of God and the whisperings He has spoken to my heart, I hope you discover a deep longing for the purposes of God. Then, as a result of these longings, I hope you resolve to make important changes in your life.

However, I do appreciate functionality. I believe we need both accurate theology and implementable practicality to effectively follow Jesus each day. I also believe we are quick to forget. If we don't apply the things we learn, we won't remember them. Just ask me if I can still do calculus! I didn't apply it and unfortunately, couldn't solve for a derivative if I tried.

My prayer is these truths become applications you live out day by day, so each chapter will end with a few processes to apply. These are not one-size-fits-all, and these are not gospel truths, but they are straightforward practices rooted in the Word of God we can implement.

SET CLEAR PARAMETERS FOR FINISHED WORK

Just as God knew when He finished creating, you too must know when your work is finished. Maybe this involves creating lists and only focusing on X number of tasks. Or maybe it's implementing a system to prioritize tasks and set aside those of less importance for another time.

A quick note on setting aside pieces of work: our hurried lifestyle has trained our minds to become anxious about incomplete tasks. However, in Matthew 6:34, Jesus commands, "Do not be anxious about tomorrow, for tomorrow will be anxious for itself. Sufficient for the day is its own trouble."

You have enough work, enough tasks, and enough to think about today. When you set aside a task for tomorrow, focus on it then . . . not today. Today has enough. You have enough. We see this with creation. God could have created everything in the first day, but He didn't. If He didn't do it all in one day, we don't need to either.

FIND YOUR "PORCH SWING"

For me, sitting on my porch swing is time intentionally set aside. Where can you go to sit without an agenda or task to complete? Where is your "porch swing"? Is it a park bench near your house? A table in the cafeteria of your workplace? The comfy chair tucked into the corner of your bedroom? Once you identify this spot, make it a priority to go, sit, and ask God to speak.

PAUSE AND LISTEN

Like Philip, we must be willing and ready to pause, listen, and obey the Lord. This process is slightly less tangible, but it starts with opening your schedule and asking God to guide your steps. If God places something on your heart, press into it. When you commit to slowing, it's amazing what God will call you to do.

Margin is the spare amount of time for God-moments. Will you implement practices to slow and create space to listen and obey His promptings?

QUESTIONS FOR REFLECTION

1. *How do you react to promptings from the Spirit? Are you willing to obey like Philip, or do you tend to hold on to your own plans and agendas?*

2. *Where can you go to sit without an agenda or task to complete (i.e., your "porch swing")?*

3. *Do you have a hard time feeling like your work is complete? If so, how can you apply the truths found in Genesis 2:1–3 to your life?*

VERSE TO MEMORIZE

Let us then with confidence draw near to the throne of grace, that we may receive mercy and find grace to help in time of need.

—HEBREWS 4:16

CHAPTER THREE

WHY CREATE MARGIN?

*Look carefully then how you walk, not as unwise but as wise,
making the best use of the time, because the days are evil.*

EPHESIANS 5:15–16

I s it really so bad to live hurried?

I'd like to think I'm good at juggling schedules. As a mom, I'm a pro at timing the school pick-up line to be able to make it to basketball practice. I can wake the baby up from her nap, feed all three boys yet another snack, and make it to the splash pad play-date. I can even say yes to coffee with a friend, unload the dishwasher, and cram four hours' worth of work into two when I really put my mind to it.

To take it further, I can look at the culture around me and identify how society seems to say more is better, efficiency is best, and success is achieved when we accomplish more. Maybe hurried living isn't so bad after all . . . right?!

We know what margin is, but why do we need to create it? Here's what Scripture says:

> Look carefully then how you walk, not as unwise but as wise,
> making the best use of the time, because the days are evil.
> (Eph. 5:15–16)

Our days are numbered. Our time is finite. Paul knew both the church at Ephesus and future believers would need to be reminded to use our time wisely; not hurriedly, but wisely.

We live in a fallen world and Scripture is clear that we have a very real enemy who seeks to steal, kill, and destroy (John 10:10). He wants nothing more than for us to be busy with all the wrong things. Here's the lie Satan has spun: If we hurry, we can do more with our time. However, here's the truth God has gently shown me: When we hurry, we elevate our selfish priorities and diminish His eternally focused promptings.

For me, often this looks like seeing things right in front of me that I feel are important or urgent and pursuing those over what I know God is telling me to do. I make a choice (sometimes without realizing it) to focus on the temporal at the sacrifice of the eternal. Overcommitment, hurry, and control affect our perspective. However, margin relieves the pressure.

This is why we create margin. This is why I'm writing this book. And this is why it's important for you to carefully examine your ways, too.

Here are five whys of the importance of creating margin that we see from Scripture.

PATIENCE PRODUCES SWEET FRUIT

My in-laws live on an 80-acre farm in a small town east of Oklahoma City. To say my boys love going to the farm is an understatement. Just saying "farm" produces a combination of joyful screams and jumping up and down, closely followed by pleading voices asking if we can go immediately.

It's no wonder why they love it. Between Minnie and Pop Pop saying yes to *nearly* every request and getting to run around freely, it's basically a little boy's dream. Not only that, but going to the farm means chasing (slightly terrified) chickens, hunting for Oklahoma mudballs, catching crawdads, fishing, feeding the cows, driving the small battery-powered Jeep, and on hot summer days, picking sand plums.

Before my in-laws moved to the farm, I had never heard of sand plums, much less tried them, but that all changed when they noticed the twiggy trees growing on their land.

One sweltering July day, the boys decided picking sand plums would be the perfect adventure. We loaded up in the Pioneer, did a little off-roading, and ended up at a thicket of trees full of ripe sand plums.

If you've ever tried to accomplish any sort of task at all with young children around, you'll understand how having more hands actually slows the process down. And when it came to picking sand plums that day, slow is an accurate description. Between their distractions and missteps, it was a sluggish process, but we ended up with several gallon buckets full of fruit.

We can learn a lot about the need to create margin from a jar of jelly. Patience and margin go hand in hand.

These ripe sand plums are fairly sweet, have a vibrant red color, and look a little like a larger-sized cherry. However, when sand plums aren't ripe, the word "tart" doesn't seem like a strong enough word to describe their taste. I'll never forget the bite my husband so lovingly made me try of an unripe sand plum!

Gathering the sand plums is really just step one though, because the end goal is always sand plum jelly. That day, my boys eagerly asked to make jelly, but the process isn't that simple. I could see the impatience written all over their faces when they realized picking sand plums wouldn't lead to an instant reward. In fact, it was November before my husband and his dad mixed that same batch of sand plums with pectin and *lots* of sugar to become a delicious jelly.

As I spread some of the jelly on bread that Christmas season, I reflected on what all went into its making: the growth of the tree, the harvest, removing the bad fruit, mixing the good fruit with the right ingredients, and lots of patience. However, the outcome was so sweet, both literally and figuratively.

I think we can learn a lot about surrendering our schedules and the need to create margin from a jar of jelly. Patience and margin go hand in hand.

We live in an instant gratification society, but jelly-making doesn't fit that mold. And sometimes, neither does God's schedule. As followers of Jesus, we create margin to ensure the figurative jelly ends up sweet and the literal rhythm of our day ends up focused on eternity. This requires a lot of patience and surrender.

Habakkuk is one man in Scripture who knew this well. Sometime between 621 and 609 BC, he prophesied to the southern kingdom of Judah. During this time the evil in Judah was rampant and the fear of God was scarce. It seemed as if the wicked prospered. Habakkuk cried out to the Lord, opening with this:

> "O LORD, how long shall I cry for help, and you will not hear?" (Hab. 1:2)

Have you ever asked God a similar question? "How long will I have to wait until ____?" "How much longer until You do ____?" We aren't a people who like to wait.

To take it even further, God's answer isn't what Habakkuk wanted.

God shared that He in fact was doing something regarding the wickedness: He was sending the Chaldeans to judge Judah (Hab. 1:5–11).

Now, not only did it seem as if wickedness was abounding, but God was sending a people group marked by cruelty to conquer His people. The Chaldeans were "dreaded and fearsome" and "all come for violence." How could this be God's plan?!

Even though this isn't what Habakkuk wanted, nor did it make sense to him, this was his response:

"I will take my stand at my watchpost and station myself on the tower, and look out to see what he will say to me, and what I will answer concerning my complaint" (Hab. 2:1).

Did you catch that? "Stand," "station," "look out." Habakkuk chose patience. He chose to wait. He chose margin. He chose to trust even when he didn't understand and didn't have the full picture (more on eternal perspective in the next chapter). And in the end, God promised He would judge the Chaldeans, bring justice to His people, and ultimately make a way for our future redemption.

Waiting on the Lord is always better.

The result of patience isn't the only reason why we need to create margin. We also create margin to put ourselves in a posture of humility and a position to serve others.

WE LOOK TO THE NEEDS OF OTHERS

A life without margin is a life that says my schedule, my plans, and my priorities are what's important. And the pressure and demands of this immediacy cause us to overlook needs that are actually present. I came face-to-face with this harsh reality one Christmas season.

As I looked at our family's bursting December calendar, my mind raced, my stomach tightened, and my hands began to sweat.[7] Not only did we have all of the normally scheduled events listed, but there were also countless holiday parties and activities. All the children had parties at school, church, and with friends; my husband had a work party and guys' dinner; and together, we had get-togethers with extended and immediate family, a neighborhood party, and a party with our church small group. It was overwhelming.

Desperate and already exhausted, I looked at my sweet husband and questioned, "Do we really need to go to all these parties?" And here's the truth: we didn't. However, it was only after I slowed down enough to look at the needs of people around me that I knew this to be true. Saying no isn't always easy.

As believers, we've been entrusted with people around us.

At the apex of my holiday overscheduling, I remember literally forcing one of my sons into the car as he cried, "Why can't we just stay hoooomeee?!" As a three-year-old, he couldn't articulate, "I'm overstimulated" or "I need some alone time," but he could (and did) have a meltdown as I forced him to go to one more "fun" thing.

Looking to the interests of others often involves sacrificing things we hold the tightest and want the most. I desperately wanted control of my schedule, to juggle it all and, honestly, to simply go have a good time with friends, but my son's actions showed me he needed something different. I had to make a choice.

I knew that if I was going to walk through this season prioritizing rest and focusing on what matters eternally, I needed to stop juggling my schedule and instead reframe my perspective.

Here's what Paul wrote, "Let each of you look not only to his own interests, but also to the interests of others" (Phil. 2:4).

As believers, we've been entrusted with people around us, and as a parent, I've been entrusted with children who have needs I'm often responsible for meeting. Sometimes, our children need us to say no for them, just as our heavenly Father often does for us.

When we say no and establish set times of margin within our schedules, we create room to take our eyes off of both ourselves and what is pressing in around us.

No matter your schedule or stage of life, life is busy. And without margin, we often stop asking God if we are doing things because He actually wants us to, or simply because we are in the habit of doing them. We fail to engage with God and forget to ask Him what He would have us do, simply because we are caught up in the busyness. Instead, margin helps us look both heavenward and outward: asking what God would have us do and what others need from us.

How often do you choose your priorities over someone's needs? Do you find yourself attempting to control, force, and/or push plans at the cost of those around you? Margin matters, and it's not optional if we want to fully obey the voice of God.

REST IS A GOOD GIFT

We create margin because rest is a good gift from our Father who loves us.

Often, in the Old Testament, we see God promise unrest as a punishment for disobedience. This idea starts in the garden.

In Genesis 3, after Adam and Eve sinned by disobeying God and eating of the tree of the knowledge of good and evil, God laid out the consequences. He cursed the serpent, told the woman her pain would be multiplied in childbearing and her desire would be contrary to her husband, and then said this to Adam:

> "Cursed is the ground because of you; in pain you shall eat
> of it all the days of your life; thorns and thistles it shall bring
> forth for you; and you shall eat the plants of the field. By the

sweat of your face you shall eat bread, till you return to the ground, for out of it you were taken; for you are dust, and to dust you shall return." (Gen. 3:17b–19)

Do you see? Pain and unending hard work are consequences. On the other hand, rest is a gift. And margin is a tool we use to prioritize the rest God gives us.

My husband, Dustin, and I have started implementing this in our parenting as well. Punch your brother? You get to go pick up doggie do instead of playing inside. Talk back to an adult? You get to spend your afternoon emptying trash cans around the house instead of chilling on the couch. Choose to directly disobey directions? You get to clean up dinner while everyone else settles down for bedtime.

When we long for rest, and find ourselves laboring instead, it doesn't take long for us to realize the consequences of our actions.

This theme continues throughout Scripture.

In Joshua, we see how the promised land is described as "a place of rest" for the Israelites (Josh. 1:13). They had been slaves in Egypt, wanderers in the desert, and yet God had a home for them. A place to rest from their turmoil and labor. A place of peace and fellowship with Him. However, because they never fully obeyed and surrendered to Him, rest was temporary and fleeting.

And yet, the Lord continued working, offering us all a true place of rest.

In Revelation 14:13, the Spirit explains how what we do on earth will follow us and says this of those who die in the Lord: "they may rest from their labors" (Rev. 14:13b).

The consequences we read about in Genesis 3 will be no more in heaven. No more physical, emotional, or spiritual labor. Instead, we will rest in His presence, a return to the intimacy and perfection of the garden. Oh, how I long for that day!

Until then, let's put in the effort it takes to create margin for rest. The consequences if we don't are detrimental.

THE LACK OF MARGIN IS A
BREEDING GROUND FOR IDOLATRY

Here's a harsh reality: if we don't create margin, our hearts and our lives can become a breeding ground for idolatry.

To fully understand this, we first need to understand what exactly an idol is.

In the Bible, we primarily see idolatry as the worship of man-made images representing false deities. So does that mean if you don't have a golden calf mounted in your living room you aren't an idolater? Not necessarily. Today, our idols may be less tangible, but they're just as evil. They are the things our heart values the most: self, money, success, control, and so on.

In an episode of the *Desiring God* podcast, John Piper defined an idol like this: "Anything that we come to rely on for some blessing, or help, or guidance, in the place of wholehearted reliance on the true and living God."[8]

I love how this definition centers on reliance! However, I think we can take it further. Idolatry involves a replacement or usurping of God, knowingly or unknowingly. It is anything we revere, trust, desire, or love equal to or above God.

Let's make it practical.

Have you relied on your financial security over trusting God's provision? Do you plan unceasingly because you don't fully rely on God's sovereignty over your day? Does your mind think about success, schedules, other relationships, _____, over God?

We have an idolatry problem.

Margin in and of itself is not the cure, but it is an effective tool in recognizing idolatry and rightly refocusing our hearts and minds on God. How?

When we slow down and intentionally lay aside time, we are disciplining ourselves to place our trust in God. It's hard to sit on a porch swing when the laundry room looks like a small tornado came through. It's not easy to get lunch with a friend in need when the demands of work are pressing in. And we all know it's a struggle to wake up in the dark when sleep is quietly whispering, "Just a few more minutes."

Idolatry is sneaky. Laundry is a sign of life in our homes, work is a good calling, and sleep is needed, but when we do those things in direct opposition to the Spirit's promptings, we reveal an idol of self. It's as if we are saying to God, "You can have the leftovers, God. I know best what I need to do at this minute."

I have a reliance issue. So often I rely on myself and my ability to plan or control or—let's be honest—manipulate situations instead of relying on God. I must create margin to remind my heart that God really is faithful and that He really is enough.

Saul had an idolatry problem, too.

Saul became the first king of Israel, a demand that came from the Israelites, not at the command of God. See any red flags yet? A couple of years into his reign, the Israelites had been fighting the Philistines and things weren't looking great for them. The Philistines had rallied, but the people of God were hiding, trembling, and waiting for instructions from the king.

Scripture doesn't tell us how Saul was feeling, but I'm sure he was stressed and everything felt urgent. But Samuel, God's prophet at the time, had told Saul to wait seven days for him to come meet Saul at Gilgal. On the seventh day, Samuel still wasn't there. Saul's men were scattering, and he was tired of waiting. In his panic, he took things into his own hands.

"So Saul said, 'Bring the burnt offering here to me, and the peace offerings.' And he offered the burnt offering. As soon as he had finished offering the burnt offering, behold, Samuel came. And Saul went out to meet him and greet him. Samuel said, 'What have you done?'" (1 Sam. 13:9–11a).

"What have you done?" Can you hear Samuel's dismay?

As established in Leviticus, only the priests were allowed to offer burnt offerings. Saul may have been king, but he was not a priest, and his actions were sinful.

Do you see the idolatry of self here? It's as if Saul is saying, "I gave You a chance God, I waited seven days, but I can't wait any longer so I'm going to take the reins here and make it work . . . You know, for the sake of the people." Saul feared losing authority, and he feared defeat. He didn't trust God to take care of them in His way. His margin wasn't enough, and his impatience cost him dearly. Saul's fears would come true: he would lose the kingdom, not because of the Philistines, but because of his heart's sinful condition.

The more I study this passage, the more I see myself in Saul. Samuel had told him to wait seven days, and Saul waited. He was obedient, but only to a point. Often, I'm willing to be obedient to a point, too. But when that point comes, the panic/fear/comparison/need to produce/control issues/etc. set in. And when they do, like Saul, I wrongfully try to take things into my own hands. Can you relate?

When you feel your heart pull toward these things, it's a good indication to stop and create enough margin for your heart to be still and look heavenward. If you don't, chances are you're creating a

> **Spiritual warfare is anything the enemy uses against us to pull our hearts and minds away from God.**

dangerous environment for idolatry to grow.

I can't end this section without mentioning the spiritual warfare at play. Spiritual warfare is anything the enemy uses against us to pull our hearts and minds away from God. The Bible teaches us that there are three elements working against us: the flesh, the world, and the enemy.

The flesh is what we've discussed in our own sinful desires and tendencies. The world is the busyness, chaos, and demands we feel pressing around us. And the enemy is Satan and those with him who are actively working against us, seeking to blind us to our own idols. The enemy is powerful, but the Bible is very clear that because of Jesus, we have power over him.

Recognize spiritual warfare exists, recognize that the enemy wants there to be idols in our lives, and then choose to order your day to keep your heart and mind abiding in Christ.

There's a final reason why we need to create margin.

WE WILL BURN OUT

A 2022 study by Barna revealed that 42 percent of pastors have considered quitting full-time ministry within the last year. Of those, 56 percent say "the immense stress of the job" has factored into their thoughts on leaving.[9]

Burnout is everywhere in our fast-paced, do-it-all, never-stop culture. Stress is prevalent, and we need margin.

You may not be a pastor, but because you're reading this book, my guess is you've been on the verge of burnout yourself. We were not created to function without intentional rest.

But our God satisfies the weary (Jer. 31:25), sustains us (Ps. 55:22), and gives us rest (Ex. 33:14). The catch? We have a part to play, and it involves taking the time to sit at His feet. It involves delegating or saying no. It means trusting the Lord to make a way when it feels like there isn't one. It means we wait, and in the waiting, we look at the One who is truly in control of it all. And it means we trust He will make *all* things work for His good, in His timing. It means we create margin.

A mentor recently told me, "There's not a problem I have that the rapture can't fix!" We had spent the morning talking about heavy things: hurting friends and family members, mental health, uncertain futures, and daily struggles. But at that moment, we laughed, reminding each other of this truth. The hurts, the struggles, and the to-do lists will all fade away one day. Eternity is coming. Don't let the lack of margin create burnout in the meantime.

PUT IT TO THE TEST

So what do you think? Is it really so bad to live hurried?

Here are a few practical applications to implement so you can answer the question for yourself.

MAKE SOME JELLY

Okay, you don't have to actually make jelly unless you really want to, but do something that has delayed gratification. Plant a garden, learn a new skill, parent a toddler (haha). The point is to wait patiently, trusting the Lord to create something sweet.

PRIORITIZE SOMEONE ELSE

Choose a day to surrender your schedule to someone else. Maybe it's a child, or maybe it's a friend or family member who could benefit from some quality time. Meet them where they are and seek to meet their needs . . . no matter the cost to you and your plans.

Identify Your Idols

Take a close look at your heart and work to find the things you rely on. The calendar on your phone? Your bank account? The need to check your email obsessively? Once you've identified it, spend some time with the Lord, repenting and asking Him to refocus your eyes on Him.

Rest with the Lord

Yep, *plan* to do nothing. Know there will always be things to accomplish, but instead, choose to spend time simply abiding in the Lord. Ask Him to speak to your heart and to refresh your mind.

We create margin as a way to slow and strip away self. It's easy to hurry, but it's so much better to wait on the Lord.

What's Next?

Up until this point we've spent time identifying the problem of hurry, control, and trying to do it all. And if you're used to hurrying and constantly trying to get to the next thing, you're probably anxiously waiting to move from identifying the problem to implementing a solution (ironic right?). I'm with you. I can even picture my husband lovingly rolling his eyes at me every time I ask, "Can't you just fix it now?" at any little problem or hang-up.

As we move into the next part of this book, you'll notice a shift from the "what" and the "why" to the "how." I don't have fix-it-all-right-now solutions to offer you, but I do have processes and tools the Lord has shown me as I've learned to slow down and surrender my schedule to Him. These tools are founded in Scripture and will require a laying down of self over and over and over. Don't stop here; keep going and ask God to give you "ears to hear."

QUESTIONS FOR REFLECTION

1. *When you have to wait, how do you respond? Do you choose patience like Habakkuk, or do you tend to take things into your own hands like Saul?*

2. *Can you identify a time when you've prioritized your plans at a cost to someone else? What can you change to avoid this in the future?*

3. *In what areas of your life do you feel burnt out? What practical steps can you take today to refocus your eyes on eternity?*

VERSE TO MEMORIZE

Look carefully then how you walk, not as unwise but as wise, making the best use of the time, because the days are evil.

—EPHESIANS 5:15–16

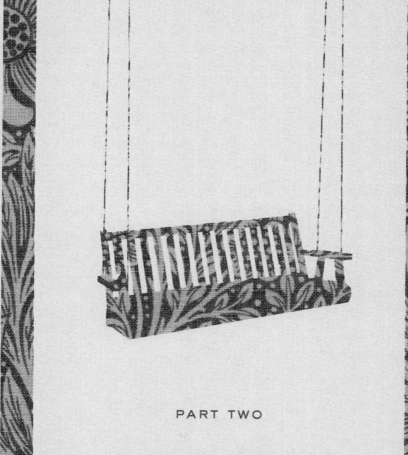

PART TWO

MAKE ROOM
FOR HIM

CHAPTER FOUR

IN LIGHT OF
ETERNITY

Set your minds on things that are above,
not on things that are on earth.

COLOSSIANS 3:2

A s we were knocking on our friend's front door, I could see confusion quickly turn to determination on the furrowed brow of my oldest son's face.

My middle son, peering through the small side window of their house, was insistent there was no one home. But my older son, tall enough to look through the larger front door window, could see the figure of a person walking toward the door and knew someone would arrive shortly. Their differing views revealed two separate pictures.

Have you ever noticed how two people can look at the same thing and see something completely different? This isn't only true of visual images. It's also true of our experiences, worldview, and circumstances.

For example, someone born and raised in New York City may simply find the subway a necessary means of transportation. But for someone who has never been to a large city, the crowded subway may seem like an exciting source of adventure, and even fun.

Our perspective matters.

How often do you think about eternity? Do you see your day through the lens of heaven?

If there's any one truth you cling to from this book, I could make a case for this being the most important. Living unhurried, relinquishing control, and surrendering our plans only makes sense and becomes truly possible when our perspective is rightly placed on eternity.

How often do we insist what we see is truth, when in reality, like my middle son, we can't see the whole picture? Or how often do we view something meant for our good with disinterest or even disdain, like a New Yorker who despises the subway?

If we truly want to become Christlike, we must shift our perspective heavenward. Our mission is clear only when viewed through the lens of eternity. This requires an intimate knowledge of His Word so that we can put on the mind of Christ as we go about our days.

I distinctly remember one day when in the midst of the busyness the Lord used His Word to help me shift my thinking toward eternal things. It looked a little like this:

I had intentions of getting up early and spending time with the Lord. Instead, I overslept after being up with a sick baby through the night. The Spirit whispered, "The steadfast love of the LORD never ceases; his mercies never come to an end; they are new every morning; great is your faithfulness" (Lam. 3:22–23).

As the day went on, I got caught up in not only what I needed to do that day, but also in what I needed to do in the upcoming days, and I became overwhelmed. I heard, "Therefore do not be anxious about tomorrow, for tomorrow will be anxious for itself. Sufficient for the day is its own trouble" (Matt. 6:34).

Later, I met up with a close friend who often has different views than I do. When I started to speak out of frustration, God said, "My dear brothers and sisters, take note of this: Everyone should be quick to listen, slow to speak and slow to become angry, because human anger does not produce the righteousness that God desires" (James 1:19–20 NIV).

Finally, as the busyness of the day slowed and I headed home, I saw the most beautiful Oklahoma sunset. My heart stirred with these words: "The heavens declare the glory of God; the skies proclaim the work of His hands" (Ps. 19:1 NIV).[10]

This chapter is designed to explain how to live moment by moment in light of eternity. So when the laundry is overflowing, the work emails are piling up, and the kids are demanding attention *now*, everything within us can still reflect Christ.

This shift starts in our hearts, souls, and minds.

WHAT'S INSIDE?

What are you thinking about right now? The words on this page? What you "should" be doing instead of reading? Everything going on around you? Something else?

Our minds are continually at work and constantly jumping from one thought to the next to the next. Our minds are a battleground for our daily sanctification. We don't naturally think and dwell only on what honors God. Unfortunately, because of our sin nature, we have work to do when it comes to filtering the filth out of our brains and fortifying our minds against that which hinders us.

Scripture reminds us of this multiple times:

In Philippians 4:8 (NIV), Paul reminds us of what we should allow into our minds:

> Finally, brothers and sisters, whatever is true, whatever is noble, whatever is right, whatever is pure, whatever is lovely, whatever is admirable—if there is anything excellent or praiseworthy— think about such things.

Colossians 3:2 directs our thinking upward:

> Set your minds on things that are above, not on things that are on earth.

Isaiah 26:3 reminds us what the result of keeping our mind on God is:

> You keep him in perfect peace whose mind is stayed on you, because he trusts in you.

And Romans 8:6 notes the consequences of failing to keep our minds on God:

> For to set the mind on the flesh is death, but to set the mind on the Spirit is life and peace.

This list is by no means exhaustive, but it solidifies this truth: following Jesus includes following Him with our minds. It begins with training and disciplining our minds for action. We will live out what we think and believe.

During Jesus' ministry on earth, a scribe approached Jesus and asked Him which commandment was the most important. Listen to His answer:

> "The most important is, 'Hear, O Israel: The Lord our God, the Lord is one. And you shall love the Lord your God with all your heart and with all your soul and with all your mind and with all your strength.'" (Mark 12:29–30)

I believe, like everything Jesus said, He was intentional here. Notice the order. He says we are to love with our strength last. The first three (heart, soul, and mind) are all internal, and it's only when our inner self is loving as God commanded that our outer self (our strength) will display true love as well.

We can try to love God and love people, but if it's not birthed out of a heart for Him, our true self will quickly be revealed. We may be putting on an act or we may be deceived or distracted. Either way, this often looks like bitterness, pride, burnout, or depression. We can't fake it before the Lord; He knows our hearts, souls, and minds.

THE MIND OF CHRIST

Today, not only does God know our thoughts, but He has given us the Spirit to help guide, purify, and renew our minds. We simply must ask and seek His guidance at each point of the day.

Here's the good news: when we are faithful to ask, God is faithful to provide. And in this case, He's provided abundantly. We don't just have help when it comes to disciplining our minds, we actually have the mind of Christ.

First Corinthians 2:16 says this: "For who has understood the mind of the Lord so as to instruct him? But we have the mind of Christ."

I remember reading this verse several years ago and picturing some goofy cartoon brain transplant taking place where the surgeon with oversized animated hands unscrews the top of his patient's head like he's opening a jar of pickles. He then takes the pink, fake-looking brain out and tosses it aside, only to drop in a brand-new beautiful, unflawed brain, quickly screwing the top of the head back on. The patient then sits up and climbs off the table with a

> **Every thought is meant to align with God's plan for the world. We see with His eyes, listen with His ears, and think with His mind.**

ginormous cheesy grin plastered on his face. Easy peasy.

I don't think this is what God means here, and maybe I've been hanging around with preschoolers too much, but this silly picture holds some, albeit far-stretched, insight into what this means for us.

"We have the mind of Christ." After we receive the Holy Spirit, our old self (including the mind) is gone. Now, every thought is meant to align with God's plan for the world. We see with His eyes, listen with His ears, and think with His mind. It's this eternal perspective that aligns us with the Lord's purposes and plans.

In his book *Mere Christianity*, C. S. Lewis says this about eternal perspective:

> "Christianity asserts that every individual human being is going to live forever. . . . There are a good many things which would not be worth bothering about if I were going to live only seventy years, but which I had better bother about very seriously if I am going to live forever."[11]

Dwelling on heaven will change everything.

But, because we are living in a spiritual war zone and waiting for Christ's return, this eternal perspective doesn't come naturally. We must continually fight to keep our minds on Christ. This means if we are going to live with our eyes on eternity, we must discipline our minds and yield to the Spirit. Here are a few practical ways to get started:

Know the Truth

The old quote "knowledge is power" is true when it comes to fortifying our minds. At every moment our emotions and circumstances are fighting for space in our minds, but it's the truth of the Word we need to make room for. God made us to have emotions and feelings, so having them isn't bad or sinful, but we must not become slaves to them. We combat emotional instability by knowing and clinging to truth. This means knowing that what God says is imperative, which involves reading your Bible, memorizing Scripture, and meditating on what you have seen to be true.

Watch What Goes In

Next, be wise about what you allow to enter your mind. We don't always have full control of this, but we do have control over the shows we watch, the music we listen to, and the places we choose to go. Know the danger zones and do what you need to do to avoid them.

However, especially for those of us those of us who are prone to legalism, remember that the Bible tells us we have freedom in Christ. Romans 14:22 says, "The faith that you have, keep between yourself and God. Blessed is the one who has no reason to pass judgment on himself for what he approves." Be fully convinced in your own mind (see Rom. 14:5b). Don't let legalism keep you from doing what God has called you to do, and don't let the things of this world become a part of who you are.

Remove and Replace

To discipline your mind, work on removing what doesn't honor God and replacing it with thoughts that do. Use Philippians 4:8 as a measuring stick, and if something isn't true, honorable, just, pure, lovely, commendable, or excellent, acknowledge this and work to think about things that are.

With the addition of a fourth child in our family, I've felt a little spread thin when it comes to giving each of them individual attention. Recently, when I asked him to help take on some additional responsibilities, my oldest son objected with, "You do those things for

Disciplining our minds isn't easy. In fact, it's really hard. It takes practice and commitment day by day.

everyone else, but not for me. You want it to be harder for me!" My first question to him was, "Is that true?" Then I helped him list a few true things about our relationship, such as "I love you" and "I value your help." His mind was quick to turn toward lies when his emotions were heightened.

And, I realized, mine were too. When I was feeling inadequate as a mom, I had to choose to stop those thoughts, and remind myself of truths from the Lord. Truths like "God's equipped me for the role He's called me to" and "He's supplied the strength I need for each moment of the day."

Disciplining our minds isn't easy. In fact, it's really hard. It takes practice and commitment day by day, but we aren't alone. Ask the Spirit to guide your mind and keep your eyes on Him.

An important reminder: Obedience in the area of disciplining our minds can seem overwhelming, as we live in a fallen world where mental illness and chemical imbalance are prevalent. Disciplining our minds and following Jesus with our hearts, soul, and mind is a command to all believers. Seeking godly counsel and taking advantage of the vast resources we have can help us find moment-by-moment victory in becoming more Christlike. Extend grace to yourself and others, acknowledge shortcomings, and ask the Lord to provide the necessary resources day by day.

If fortifying our minds is the first step in living with an eternal perspective, knowing what awaits us in heaven is next.

HEAVEN VERSUS EARTH

I have so many questions about heaven, and sometimes it feels like seeking answers just leads to more questions. But what I do know is that over and over Scripture contrasts heaven and earth, what we can't see to what we can, and what we don't know to what we do.

When things on earth feel temporary and meaningless, we can remember heaven is permanent and lasting. When things on earth feel broken, we can remember heaven is indestructible. And when things on earth feel painful, taxing, and hard, we can remember heaven is without flaw.

None of us know the number of our days, but we can look at heaven full of hope, longing, and expectancy no matter what today holds.

If we are going to slow down and create margin by focusing our eyes on heaven, here are three important things to know about how heaven differs from earth.

Heaven Is Forever

This may not be a revolutionary thought, but it's worth dwelling on because we are so quick to forget this world is fading away. Your job won't last, your kids will grow up, and the season you are in will end . . . but heaven won't.

Here's what Paul reminded the church in Corinth:

> So we do not lose heart. Though our outer self is wasting away, our inner self is being renewed day by day. For this light momentary affliction is preparing for us an eternal

weight of glory beyond all comparison, as we look not to the things that are seen but to the things that are unseen. For the things that are seen are transient, but the things that are unseen are eternal. (2 Cor. 4:16–18)

Have you ever noticed how the things right in front of you are what seem the most urgent? Scripture tells us they are "transient" or "temporary." These seemingly urgent things won't last. But the "unseen," or the things God is concerned with, things that impact eternity, are unending.

If we can remember this as we go about our days, it changes everything. It doesn't mean the demands of life won't come, and it doesn't mean urgent tasks won't arise, but it does mean we will be able to see these things for what they are: temporary blips that provide opportunities to impact eternity.

Heaven Is Indestructible

We affectionately call our second son "Wreck-It Ralph." From the time he could scoot around, he was out to destroy. It's not malicious; he just loves to hit, smash, kick, jump on, dive in, and knock over just about anything that's around him. And as you can imagine, this isn't his siblings' favorite quality. He's knocked down block towers, accidentally broken valued possessions (just ask my husband to tell the story about how a thrown Lincoln Log cracked our TV), and ripped school papers more times than I'd like to admit.

When my oldest son becomes frustrated by his younger brother's actions, I often remind him that our possessions here on this earth won't last . . . whether they are destroyed by his brother or not.

This isn't the case in heaven. Take a look at what Jesus says in this passage:

"Do not lay up for yourselves treasures on earth, where moth and rust destroy and where thieves break in and steal, but lay up for yourselves treasures in heaven, where neither moth nor rust destroys and where thieves do not break in and steal. For where your treasure is, there your heart will be also." (Matt. 6:19–21)

No moths, no rust, no thieves. In heaven, our treasures last.

But what are our treasures? Or what should they be at least?

I love how the renowned nineteenth-century English preacher Charles Spurgeon answered these questions:

"Whatever we make to be our treasure will be sure to become the attraction of our heart. If we accumulate earthly riches, our hearts will by degrees be tied up in our money-bags; and, on the other hand, if our chief possessions are in heavenly things, our hearts will rise into the higher and more spiritual region. The position of the heart is sure to be affected by the place where the treasure is laid up."[12]

Don't let hurry, control, and over-planning direct the "attractions of your heart" earthward. Instead, prioritize margin, shift your eyes toward heaven, and position your heart to treasure God and the gifts He gives. This can never be destroyed.

Heaven Is Perfect

Living with an eternal perspective becomes a little easier when we remember the perfection of heaven.

Revelation gives us a small glimpse into this. Read the passage below and note what you learn about heaven:

And I heard a loud voice from the throne saying, "Behold, the dwelling place of God is with man. He will dwell with them, and they will be his people, and God himself will be with them as their God. He will wipe away every tear from their eyes, and death shall be no more, neither shall there be mourning, nor crying, nor pain anymore, for the former things have passed away." (Rev. 21:3–4)

What did you find? Here's my list: God will dwell with us. He will wipe our tears from our eyes. There will be no death in heaven, nor will there be *any* mourning or crying . . . nor any pain. Heaven will be different from earth because "the former things [will have] passed away."

Do you realize the magnitude of this description? It sounds pretty good to me!

I don't love the unknown, and so sometimes dwelling on heaven is hard for me. But when I shift to the things I do know, God is so gracious to remind me this is the place He's designed for those who follow Him. We will physically be with Him. And since we only see and experience life with our limited, earthly perspective, it's difficult to comprehend that all He's prepared for us will be perfect.

Life is hard, but heaven's not. When we slow down and intentionally spend time with the Lord, we become more and more prone to remember this day by day, hour by hour.

There's a final key to living in light of eternity.

THE GLORY IS GOD'S

Everything God has done, is doing, and will do is for the purpose of His glory.

But what does this mean? To glorify God is to exalt His character and attributes, to praise Him for what He has done and will do, to trust Him with our lives and the lives of those we love, to revere Him, to obey His Word, and to seek to honor Him as Lord in every area of our life. It means we take the opportunities He places before us to make Him and His name known in our speech and in our actions.

The Bible reveals this idea on every page. Ever since the fall in Genesis 3, God has been at work, glorifying Himself by providing a way for salvation (Jesus), redeeming His people, and equipping them (through the Holy Spirit) to honor God with their lives.

And here's how this ties in: if we will surrender control, live slower, and remember this in each moment of the day, our plans will fall in line with His purposes. Our lives will be centered around giving Him the glory He deserves.

There is a basic catechism question in Dwayne Milioni's book *A New Baptist Catechism* Dustin and I teach our kids. We ask: "Why did God make me?" And the answer is simply this: "God made me to bring Him glory."[13]

The book of Ezekiel shows this idea of God's desire for His glory over and over, with the statement "they shall know that I am the LORD" appearing over sixty times in this book alone.

> **God acts, over and over and over again, for the purpose of His glory. What about you? Are you acting for your glory or for His?**

Take a look at this example:

> "It is not for your sake, O house of Israel, that I am about to act, but for the sake of my holy name, which you have profaned among the nations to which you came. And I will vindicate the holiness of my great name, which has been profaned among the nations, and which you have profaned among them. And the nations will know that I am the LORD, declares the Lord GOD, when through you I vindicate my holiness before their eyes." (Ezek. 36:22–23)

God's people had disobeyed and dishonored Him nearly every step of the way. Why did God promise to redeem, bring them back, and forgive? "For the sake of my [God's] holy name." And so "the nations will know that I [God] am the LORD."

God acts, over and over and over again, for the purpose of His glory.

What about you? Are you acting, over and over and over again, for your glory or for His glory? It's easy to get these mixed up. It takes intentional practice to take ourselves out of the main picture and purpose ourselves for His glory alone. Here are a couple questions to help you navigate this: Do your days revolve around God and His purposes? Or are you so busy that you forget and, intentionally or not, allow your schedule to blind you to the work of eternity?

Oh friend, look up! His glory is here! Don't miss it.

WHERE ARE YOU LOOKING?

So let's return to the question from early in the chapter: How often do you think about eternity? Do you see your day through the lens of heaven?

Here are a couple of practical applications to put to the test as you take the next step today.

USE PHILIPPIANS 4:8 TO MEASURE YOUR THOUGHTS

Following Jesus with our minds can be an overwhelming and vague concept to try to implement if we don't have a practical plumb line to use. Thankfully, God graciously gave us one in Philippians 4:8. Work to memorize this verse, and anytime things like doubts, fears, anxiety, or control creep in, discipline yourself to ask: Is this true? Honorable? Just? Pure? Lovely? Commendable? Excellent? And then ask God to shift your thoughts to things that are.

LISTEN TO HYMNS/PRAISE SONGS ABOUT HEAVEN

My Grandpa Charlie's favorite hymn was "Because He Lives."[14] A few years before he went home to be with the Lord, he and my grandma left the small west Texas town they had lived in for over seventy years and moved into an assisted living facility near my parents in Oklahoma. On one of their last Sundays at the small Baptist church where they worshiped and served for all those years, the music minister led the congregation in this classic. It may have been the realization that this was one of the last times worshiping in the small chapel there, or maybe the power of the lyrics, but either way, as my grandpa sang the familiar words, unexpected tears streamed down his face. In a deep, strong yet shaky voice, with his soft, worn hands raised, he sang the last verse describing the victory we will experience when the pain of earth has passed away and we enter glory to dwell with our Father, the reigning King.

Not only are the words of this triumphant hymn true, but they should shift our thinking of heaven, and if you're not familiar with it, it's well worth looking up. Whether you are eighteen or eighty, our time is finite. But we can face this knowing we have the hope of heaven. In the chaos and in the margins, let's be people who ask God to help us fix our eyes on what matters eternally.

READ SCRIPTURE LOOKING FOR GOD'S GLORY

Every book of the Bible points to the glory of God. Take some time as you read Scripture to intentionally look for instances where God reveals why He's acting the way He is or verses where He explicitly points to His glory. Underline them as you read.

Eternal perspective isn't natural and isn't always easy, but it is a critical component in learning to live a slower life focused on God's purposes above your plans.

QUESTIONS FOR REFLECTION

1. *Do you struggle to keep your mind on Jesus? How can you shift your thinking from the things of earth to the things of heaven?*

2. *What are some additional ways heaven differs from earth? How should these differences affect the way we live now?*

3. *In what ways do you see yourself acting for your glory instead of God's glory? How can you hand this back over to Him? Where have you seen God acting for the sake of His glory in your life?*

VERSE TO MEMORIZE

Set your minds on things that are above,
not on things that are on earth.

—COLOSSIANS 3:2

CHAPTER FIVE

THE LORD'S PLANS PREVAIL

Many are the plans in a person's heart,
but it is the LORD's purpose that prevails.

PROVERBS 19:21 (NIV)

I walked into my tiny bedroom in the beat-up rental house I shared with friends my final year at Texas A&M, and it started to sink in: I was getting married, and this meant I had a wedding to plan.

A few hours earlier, Dustin had proposed. One of the last words used to describe my husband would be "planner." He is easy-going, the type B to my type A, and a picture of faith and steadfastness. I've yet to see an external circumstance rock him. But for all of his amazing qualities, planning isn't one of them.

You may have picked up on this, but I am quite the opposite. For as long as I can remember, one of the first thoughts to cross my mind when I wake up is, "What's the plan for today?" I plan out vacations, I plan my kids' days pretty much to the hour, and I make plans for everything from meetings to playdates to meals. Plans provide comfort and structure to my day.

However, while plans may provide a level of predictability, at their core, plans are an attempt to control what happens around us. The tighter we hold on to our plans, the less we focus our eyes on the One who is really in control of it all. This doesn't mean we never make plans, or simply live on a whim, but it does mean we ask the Lord for His wisdom and discernment first. Then, we hold on to our plans with open hands, acknowledging that the Lord's plans are far greater than our own.

It was in this season of our engagement when the Lord started to reveal these truths to me. After the adrenaline died down and the engagement party guests cleared out, I was left with a beautiful new ring on my finger and a head spinning with wedding ideas. To complicate things, Dustin was preparing for a nine-month deployment to Afghanistan with the army and was leaving within the month.

However, in my mind, this too could be planned around.

As the months passed, I quickly learned the United States Army cared very little about my wedding plans (something about having bigger tasks at hand). Soon, my desire to plan a wedding and my tight hold on control stepped into a boxing ring with my fiancé's current mission. I won't tell you who came out victorious, but I bet you can take a guess.

Suddenly, our relationship became strained. Phone calls and Skype sessions were filled with frustration, tears, and anger when he had to leave unexpectedly, couldn't talk for long, technology failed, or he wanted to talk about things other than the color of my bridesmaid dresses (teal for anyone who wants to know).

God was using the hardships and brokenness that marked this season, but it took time and a new perspective to see all He was doing. Often, as Dustin and I look back on this season, we reflect on the Lord's goodness. A goodness I, unfortunately, turned a blind eye to at the time.

As I hung on to control, God took it from me and told me His plan was better. As Dustin and I pushed and strained and clung to the love we had for each other, we learned how to communicate, making our first year of marriage a dream (mostly). And as my plans failed time and time again, the Lord's plans prevailed.

> **Have you ever been there? Missing out on the goodness of God while waiting for life to start?**

Instead of the year I had planned and anticipated, God used Dustin to share the gospel and minister to broken men overseas. The Lord placed younger college women in my life whom I was able to disciple and invest in. He sent me to Brazil after graduation to increase my faith and open my eyes to a slower pace of life. He provided jobs, an apartment, and yes, all the details for a wedding.

So much of this occurred outside of our own plans. When I thought I was just waiting for time to pass and for our life to start, God was working.

Have you ever been there? Missing out on the goodness of God while waiting for life to start? Maybe it's waiting for graduation, the perfect job, a spouse, a child, retirement, etc. Whatever it is, don't let the waiting make you miss what God's doing now.

Without my knowing it, God was teaching me about the way He works in the waiting, in the extra spaces, in the unplanned. Through His Word, God slowly called me to slow down and trained my eyes to look for Him at work. He also reminded me that He prepares and equips His followers for the task at hand.

Many divine encounters detailed in the Word of God occur only when someone detours from their plan or experiences the unexpected.

MOSES AND THE BURNING BUSH

We read in Exodus 3 that after murdering an Egyptian, fleeing to Midian, and marrying Zipporah, Moses made his plans for the day. His plans involved sheep, lots of sheep. Exodus 3 begins with Moses leading the flock—not a quick activity to check off the to-do list—through the wilderness toward Horeb, the "mountain of God." Maybe you know what happened next: seeing a flame, Moses went nearer to inspect what was burning. He saw a bush that appeared to be on fire, yet . . . he probably crept closer to get a better look. To his surprise, instead of a pile of burnt wood and ashes, he saw a healthy bush burning—actually on fire, but still living, not eaten up by the flames.

So often in this story, we get caught up picturing the burning bush and trying to imagine what it might have looked like, and we miss what Moses does.

"I will turn aside to see this great sight, why the bush is not burned" (Ex. 3:3). Moses turned aside. In other words, he stuck around and checked it out. He stopped, looked, and realized though the bush was burning, it was not consumed. Moses gave the bush his full attention.

He could've kept going, thinking to himself how he doesn't have time to stop. He could've ignored the fire, thinking it was dangerous or someone else's problem. He could've even turned around to go get someone else to come and see.

Instead, he turned aside. And it was only when the Lord saw that Moses turned—that he had gone over to look—that He called out to him. "Moses, Moses!"

He responded, "Here I am."

What do you do when the Lord speaks? Do you stick around and check it out? Moses' plans were secondary to what the Lord had planned for him.

When you sense the Spirit urging you to start a conversation with the woman in the grocery store who looks lonely, do you stop and turn to her, or do you keep pushing your cart on your mission to grab what you need and leave as quickly as possible? When your child asks an important question, or a spiritual one, do you stop, listen, pray, and answer intentionally, or do you brush it off and make a mental note to address it later? When God asks you to give that extra twenty-dollar bill in your wallet, do you stop and give immediately and joyfully, or do you resist, making excuses for why you need it more?

To actively apply the full Word of God, it's important to note Moses may have turned toward the burning bush right away and said, "Here I am," but when he discovered the task God had for him, it took time for him to agree and obey.

Moses questioned his abilities in Exodus 3:11: "Who am I that I should go to Pharaoh and bring the children of Israel out of Egypt?"

Moses feared what others would think in Exodus 4:1: "They will not believe me or listen to my voice, for they will say, 'The LORD did not appear to you.'"

Moses made excuses in Exodus 4:10: "Oh, my Lord, I am not eloquent, either in the past or since you have spoken to your servant, but I am slow of speech and of tongue."

And when God had countered all his objections, he finally asked to just stay where he was comfortable: "Oh, my Lord, please send someone else" (Ex. 4:13).

It's not always easy to abandon our plans for God's plans. There will always be excuses, hesitations, fears; and often, they will be legitimate. But God's plans are always better. In His sovereignty, God knows what His people need and will always provide.

When Moses finally decided to lay His plans and fears aside and obey the Lord, God used him to deliver Israel from bondage in

Egypt. How will God use you when you finally lay your plans and fears aside?

Let's look at another biblical example.

SAUL ON THE ROAD TO DAMASCUS

Saul had a clear and well-laid plan, and he was pretty good at implementing it.

> Saul, still breathing threats and murder against the disciples of the Lord, went to the high priest and asked him for letters to the synagogues at Damascus, so that if he found any belonging to the Way, men or women, he might bring them bound to Jerusalem. (Acts 9:1–2)

He had a mission: persecute the disciples of Jesus. He gained support from the high priest. And he had a plan: find followers of the Way, that is, those who were disciples of Jesus, bind them, and bring them to Jerusalem. Nice and clear-cut. No snags.

What happens next is a clear picture of what it is to experience the unexpected.

> Now as he went on his way, he approached Damascus, and suddenly a light from heaven shone around him. And falling to the ground, he heard a voice saying to him, "Saul, Saul, why are you persecuting me?" And he said, "Who are you, Lord?" And he said, "I am Jesus, whom you are persecuting." (Acts 9:3–5)

Saul had a plan, but ultimately, the Lord's plan prevailed. When God spoke, Saul totally and immediately abandoned his plans outright. Instead, he walked forward into God's plans for his life. God completely transformed him. When it comes to letting go of our plans, sometimes God stops us and asks us to turn and respond as Moses did. Other times, like in Saul's case, He uses circumstances, events, people, and divine encounters to bring us to our knees, disrupt our well-laid plans, and change our paths.

Either way, we can choose to continue planning, striving, and working for ourselves, or we can choose to lay aside whatever we are occupied with at that moment to follow Jesus.

Whenever I struggle with this, I go back to Matthew 6:25–34 and read how God feeds the birds of the air even though they don't sow, reap, or gather, and how beautifully He clothes the lilies of the field even though they don't do the work of making themselves lovely. It's not wrong to plan, but it is wrong to hold so tightly to those plans that we worry and fail to trust the One who provides for our daily needs. Bible teacher Kelly Minter describes this verse like this: "The point is that we humans have the faculties to plan, save, invest, and freeze the ground beef until we need it for lasagna. The birds can't do this! They live day-to-day, worm-to-appetizing-worm, not because of their planning abilities but because Creator God takes care of their needs."[15]

God takes care of our needs. We don't need to plan as though He doesn't.

SCRIBBLES AND THE SOVEREIGNTY OF GOD

After I began to slow down and stop planning every millisecond of my life, my perspective changed.

Before this, a long line at the grocery store was frustrating. After, it was still slightly annoying, but also became an opportunity to pray for the people around me. Before, running into a friend was cutting into the time I had allotted for something else. After, it became an opportunity to check in and show love. Before, my kids' naturally slow pace of life was inconvenient. After, their viewpoints have taught me to find beauty in the small, ordinary things.

I began to recognize the Lord's hand in everyday moments throughout my day. As I perceived His hand, I also began to discern His purposes. Out of all the aspects of His character, He started revealing to me His sovereignty.

But what exactly does "sovereign" mean? And how does it apply to pursuing the Lord's plans, creating margin, and living in obedience?

John Piper, a well-known theologian, author, and pastor, explains God's sovereignty this way: "God has the rightful authority, the freedom, the wisdom, and the power to bring about everything that he intends to happen. And therefore, everything he intends to come about does come about. Which means, God plans and governs all things."[16]

I really didn't want to write about the sovereignty of God. It felt (and still feels) intimidating and incomprehensible. However, one summer afternoon, the Lord used my son to help give me insight and understanding.

"You'll just have to wait and see, Momma," my three-year-old exclaimed when I asked what he was creating. After a few minutes of carefully selecting colors, considering placement, and focusing intently, he proudly held up a page full of what looked like scribbles to me. However, in his vivid imagination, the squiggles at the top were fighter jets and the chaotic, mismatched lines I saw were actually farm animals waving at the plane above.

I needed his help to see and to know what the strokes he worked hard on were made to create.

Oftentimes, it feels like a lot of what is going on around us is scribbles and chaotic lines. Uncertainty, a lack of clarity, changing plans, and a world in chaos seems to be the norm. Our plans are often a poor attempt at controlling the "scribbles."

However, those "scribbles" aren't scribbles to God, and what seems like chaos is still a means to accomplish God's purposes and plans. He sees the picture because He created it. Reliance on Him helps us to interpret and understand the lines as they're drawn.

To boil it down, the Lord's plans prevail because He is sovereign.

God plans and governs all things. He planned the burning bush, He planned the encounter with Saul on the road to Damascus, and He has planned every moment of your life.

How can we know this to be true? God's Word tells us in Isaiah 46:9–11.

> "I am God, and there is no other;
>> I am God, and there is none like me,
> declaring the end from the beginning
>> and from ancient times things not yet done,
> saying, 'My counsel shall stand,
>> and I will accomplish all my purpose,' . . .
> I have spoken, and I will bring it to pass;
>> I have purposed, and I will do it."

And yet, we have a choice. We can choose to trust in His plan and join in His work, or we can choose to continue striving and fighting for control.

We see God's sovereignty and mankind's free will throughout Scripture and in our lives today.

This is not a book of free will versus sovereignty; it would need to be a much larger book for that. It is a book about laying aside our plans for the purposes of God, which means it is essential we know, understand, and trust God and His sovereignty. In the same way, we must understand we have the freedom to make our own choices. We are not robots!

In *Trusting God,* Jerry Bridges says this: "We must not misconstrue God's sovereignty so as to make people mere puppets, so we must not press man's freedom to the point of limiting God's sovereignty."[17]

We see God's sovereignty and mankind's free will throughout Scripture and in our lives today. We do have the ability to make our own choices, but we must also recognize these choices have ramifications. What we choose and how we use our will makes an eternal difference.

Let me also add that if you're having a hard time wrapping your mind around these truths, it's okay. While on this earth, there may be things we cannot reconcile or fully understand; however, how we respond to these truths matters. We can continue resisting, or we can lay aside our objections, praise Him, and humbly submit to our sovereign God.

In my living room, the poem "Life Is but a Weaving" hangs next to a small tapestry to remind me who is in control of my life. Written by Grant Colfax Tullar but popularly quoted by Corrie ten Boom, a woman who helped many Jews escape the Nazis during the Holocaust, it describes how the front and back of a tapestry look vastly different. Often, we only see the back, with its messy and dark threads. But God sees the front and knows those dark threads were just as needed as the bright and beautiful ones in order to create a masterpiece. It's up to us to trust His skilled hand with our lives.

AS YOU ARE GOING

Choosing to join God in His sovereign work happens in the everyday moments of our lives.

When we choose to live unhurried and intentionally create margin, we are creating opportunities for detours. In other words, if we are less focused on getting from point A to point B in a hurry, we will be more willing, and even eager, to take the scenic bypass.

Jesus gives us the perfect example in John 9. Verse 1 says this, "As he [Jesus] passed by, he saw a man blind from birth."

Jesus was on the move, but having a goal or destination in mind did not keep Him from seeing and meeting the needs of those around Him. Not only was He open to "detours," but He was looking for them. And often, they occurred "as He was going."

As the text continues, we read that Jesus healed this man physically (v. 7) and spiritually (v. 38). Jesus' obedience to the Father's promptings changed a man's eternity.

How about you? Are your eyes open to people around you? Are you willing to stop in the middle of your day to meet the needs of others and to engage in eternally impactful conversations?

As we choose to slow down and open our eyes, we choose to be more in tune to the promptings of the Spirit.

Here are a few practices to implement "as you are going."

AVOID BEING RUSHED

I of all people can tell you this is much easier said than done (just ask my kids how often I say, "Hurry, we don't want to be late!"). However, if you know you need to leave the house by nine, plan to leave by 8:45 or even 8:30. Allotting extra time will not only help you create margin, but it will also give you opportunities to lift your eyes and look around.

KNOW THE FATHER'S VOICE

Next, if we are to respond when the Lord asks us to stop or detour, we must know His voice. This involves spending time in prayer and reading His Word. The more time we spend with Him, the easier it will be to discern His will.

PRACTICE

Once you become accustomed to busyness and hurry, slowing down takes practice. Start small. Plan to take a walk around your neighborhood and simply look around and pray for the people you see. Pick one event to arrive early and see if the Lord tugs on your heart in some way.

God is sovereign and His plans have and will prevail. Will you slow down and join Him as you are going?

QUESTIONS FOR REFLECTION

1. *Have you ever detoured from your plan or experienced the unexpected? What was the result?*

2. *What are some little inconveniences in your life (e.g., long lines, slow kids) that may actually be opportunities from the Lord? How can you use these "inconveniences" to make a kingdom impact?*

3. *Should God's sovereignty affect the way you plan? Why or why not?*

VERSE TO MEMORIZE

Many are the plans in a person's heart,
but it is the LORD's purpose that prevails.

—PROVERBS 19:21 (NIV)

CHAPTER SIX

A CALL TO ABIDE

"Abide in me, and I in you. As the branch cannot bear
fruit by itself, unless it abides in the vine, neither can you,
unless you abide in me. I am the vine; you are the branches.
Whoever abides in me and I in him, he it is that bears
much fruit, for apart from me you can do nothing."

JOHN 15:4–5

I scrubbed the last dirty dish, hung up another load of unending laundry, and confirmed that the kids were finally asleep.

As the last sun rays of the day beamed through our window, I sat down next to my husband on the couch. Instantly, I started verbally processing the day, going over to-do lists, and hammering off questions regarding upcoming plans. Dustin lovingly looked at me and quietly said, "Samantha, just stop and be with me."

Be with me . . . not with an agenda or a list or a need. Just be.

Throughout the Bible, we see a similar reminder from the Lord to His people in the call to "abide."

This call to abide is a call to remain, to stay, to live, and to be held and kept continually.[18] It's the picture of a mother tenderly holding her infant, knowing dinner can wait and sleep will come eventually, but this short season with a newborn is to be treasured.

If we are to examine our ways and surrender our plans to the Lord's purposes, abiding must sit at the center. Abiding is the decision to remain so in tune with the Spirit that everything else pales in comparison.

Hudson Taylor, one of the first missionaries to inland China, explained it like this: "Abiding in Jesus isn't fixing our attention on Christ, but it is being one with Him. . . . A man is abiding just as much when he is sleeping for Jesus, as when he is awake and working for Jesus. Oh, it is a very sweet thing to have one's mind just resting there."[19]

Here's the truth: Abiding in Christ isn't just an idea or something that sounds nice to pursue, it's actually a command we see Jesus give. It's a necessity for believers who seek intimacy with the Father.

What about you? Is your mind resting on Christ? Are you pursuing intimacy with Him?

Scripture gives us insight into the importance of remaining (abiding) in Christ in John 15.

APART FROM HIM . . .

In the time leading up to Jesus' death and resurrection, He leaves the disciples with several clear and significant instructions. These instructions include loving one another (John 13:34), doing the works He does (John 14:12), looking for the coming Holy Spirit (John 14:16), and preparing for the world to be against them (John 15:19). Nestled in the middle of this list, we find His instructions to abide.

> "Abide in me, and I in you. As the branch cannot bear fruit
> by itself, unless it abides in the vine, neither can you, unless

you abide in me. I am the vine; you are the branches. Whoever abides in me and I in him, he it is that bears much fruit,
for apart from me you can do nothing." (John 15:4–5)

Did you catch that the word "abide" is used four times in these
two verses? I think it's important we tune in.

Here, we learn about a few key components of abiding.

Abiding is two-sided

Not only does Christ want us to remain in Him, but He has a desire to remain in us as well. As the Spirit dwells within, we can know
God and know His will. This brings joy, power, purpose, and peace.

Abiding serves a purpose: We are to bear fruit

The other day my son picked a flower that hadn't fully bloomed
yet. He excitedly brought it to me and asked when it would open.
Tears filled his eyes as he learned the flower would never bloom
because it needed the roots from which it had been severed.

As believers, we should know and understand our call to make
disciples and bear the fruit of the Spirit (Galatians 5). However, this
is only possible when we remain in Christ. I love how Tara Dew sim-
plifies it this way in *Overflowing Joy*: "The way to bear fruit, the way
to have joy, the way to live a life of abundance is to stay connected
and dependent on the Vine."[20]

Cutting ourselves off from the vine will lead to a fruitless life.

Abiding requires us to remove self-righteous efforts and agendas

"Apart from me you can do nothing," Jesus said. He did not say,
"Apart from me you can do some things, or only good things, or things
you think are good." He said, "Nothing." Even my good intentions,

well-meaning pursuits, and impressive-to-the-world accomplishments are meaningless apart from God.

This call to abide is a call to lie prostrate before the Lord, knowing there's nothing I can bring other than my desperate need and willing heart to be with my Savior. It is here where we die to self and learn what it is to live yielded and filled with the Spirit.

As I reflected on my husband's request to "just be with him," I realized a few truths. His words didn't belittle the work I had done or the conversations that needed to occur at some point. Instead, they were an invitation to shift my priorities. As a covenant relationship, our marriage matters eternally as we work to display Christ's love for His church. To know each other and know the purposes God has for us, we must abide with one another.

> **This call to abide is a call to lie prostrate before the Lord, knowing there's nothing I can bring other than my desperate need and willing heart to be with my Savior.**

We, too, are in a covenant relationship with Christ. Abiding with Christ shouldn't be considered optional. However, it is good, life-giving, and essential in fulfilling our calling and aligning our desires with the Father's.

When was the last time you stopped and chose to simply be with the Lord? This doesn't have to look like waking up early to find time that is quiet (although it could). Maybe it looks like choosing to sit (without your phone) on the porch while your kids play outside. Maybe it's taking a walk, or playing worship music in the car, or actually taking your lunch break, or simply turning the TV off.

That evening, thanks to my husband's prompting, I chose to sit and be. In the quiet, I realized just how much my heart needed this time with him. It was life-giving, joyful, and restorative.

Time with the Father is the same way on a magnified level. Jesus ends the instruction to abide in John 15 by explicitly stating His purpose: "These things I have spoken to you, that my joy may be in you, and that your joy may be full" (John 15:11).

Abiding leads to joy: abundant, filling, life-giving joy.

DELIGHT IN HIM

Not only does abiding lead to joy, but it also produces soul-level delight in God, our Father.

We've defined abiding as remaining, staying, living, and being held and kept continually. Delight is the result of this. Delight is a tenderness, a stirring of our affections, and a deep pleasure and contentment rooted in who God is.

As we draw near and learn to listen to the Spirit's promptings above our own plans, something supernatural happens: we begin to experience the joy of His ways. We delight in His holiness and find that we want more and more of Christ in us.

The psalmist says it this way:

> Trust in the LORD, and do good;
> > dwell in the land and befriend faithfulness.
> Delight yourself in the LORD,
> > and he will give you the desires of your heart. (Ps. 37:3–4)

The promises here are so sweet and appealing. Oh, how I desire to befriend faithfulness and allow God to shape my heart's desires. There's a critical caveat we can't overlook: our delight is to be in the Lord. Not in what He can do, not who we think He is, but in who He actually is. This is why we must slow down. This is why we must lay aside our plans for His purposes. And this is why we must abide.

If we are to truly find our delight in the Lord, there are a couple of warnings we must recognize and take heed of.

Delight Is Not a Means to an End

Be honest—have you ever thought, "If I will obey God in _____, then He will give me what I want"? Whether you admit to it or not, sometimes we live expecting God's blessings in return for our obedience. This is the "prosperity gospel." It's not what Scripture promises, and it actually robs us of delighting in God. It causes us to seek Him out because of what He can give, not because of who He is.

In *The One Year Praying Through the Bible for Your Kids*, Nancy Guthrie comments on Psalm 37:3–4:

> Delighting in God is not a means to get what we want from him. That is manipulation. Genuine affection for God is an end in itself, not the means to some further ends. Genuine delight has no ulterior motives, no additional demands. Delight says thank you to God for his many blessings such as good food to eat, a house to live in, people who love you, and a job to go to, but it also says, *I will not worship these things by demanding them from you.*[21]

We don't slow down to have a "better," less stressful life, though that may be a beneficial by-product. We slow down to tune our hearts to the Spirit. We don't abide in Christ only when we feel out of control or helpless. We abide because we long to know our Savior more. Delight is birthed from an intimacy that comes from knowing God. And as we know Him, our heart's desire becomes to be more like Him.

There's one more way Satan has twisted delight in this world.

Drawn by Turkish Delight

One of the first audiobooks I ever listened to was C. S. Lewis's *The Lion, the Witch and the Wardrobe.*[22] My mom rented it from the library for us to listen to as a family on a road trip, and I fell in love with the magical land of Narnia.

There's a point in the story where Edmund, one of the children who has found their way to Narnia, meets the White Witch. The White Witch has Narnia under a spell that makes it "always winter, but never Christmas." She is evil and is seeking the children to kill them. But when she first meets Edmund, she deceives him by acting friendly and asking him this simple question: "What would you like best to eat?"

Edmund, despite what he has heard about the dangers of the White Witch, eagerly answers with Turkish Delight (don't miss the "delight" in the name here). He loves Turkish Delight, and it seems innocent enough to accept some candy. However, what he doesn't know is that the witch placed a spell on the candy, and the more he eats, the more he wants. At one point he becomes so desperate for the candy that he is even willing to betray and endanger his siblings.

> **What is your "Turkish Delight"? Is there something in your life you are delighting in more than God?**

In the story, Turkish Delight symbolizes temptation and the way temptation makes way for sin. James warns us of this very path: "Then desire when it has conceived gives birth to sin, and sin when it is fully grown brings forth death" (James 1:15).

Desire, temptation, and delight in anything other than God may seem so innocent at first. It was just a little candy, right? However, the reality is what we desire soon fills our hearts and clouds our minds.

What about you? What is your "Turkish Delight"? Is there something in your life you are delighting in more than God? Our hearts are prone to seek delight in things that will never satisfy. However, when our delight is in the Lord, there is truly nothing sweeter.

So what do we do when we realize we've become captivated by Turkish Delight?

In the story, Edmund—who went from carefree to captive—eventually recognizes what he's done and that the White Witch is not his friend at all, but actually "bad and cruel." However, once he's rescued, he meets with Aslan, the great lion (who symbolizes Jesus). After a conversation with Aslan, Edmund reveals his change of heart by asking for forgiveness and even fighting against the White Witch.

Here's what we can take away: When our delight is misplaced, we need to slow down and recognize the error of our ways. Then, we repent and draw near to the Father. And as we draw near, our heart softens, our ways change, and we become more and more like Jesus—fighting the battles He calls us to fight.

Delight is good and sweet and life-giving, but only when our delight is in the Lord. Slow down, abide, and ask God to help you delight in Him today.

GUARD THE TREASURE

There's a final piece to slowing, delighting, and abiding in God, and it involves recognizing the value of what we've been given through Jesus. We must guard the treasure entrusted to us.

Nearby our house is a nature park full of trails my boys love to explore. Not long after my oldest could walk, I remember watching him toddle along the trail, stopping frequently to look at a bug or pick up a rock or feather. It didn't take long before I noticed his little shorts starting to look saggy, pulled down by the weight of what was in his pockets. Slightly afraid of the answer, I asked him what was inside. And in his sweet, baby voice, he matter-of-factly replied, "Twe-sures."

I didn't even know he knew the word "treasure," much less what it meant at his age, but in his little mind, he believed what he was collecting was valuable. His pockets were full of dirt-covered pebbles, shells, sticks, and grass. Clearly not valuable by my standards (and actually a detriment to my laundry later that day), but invaluable to him.

See how Paul charges his protégé Timothy:

> Guard [with greatest care] and keep unchanged, the treasure [that precious truth] which has been entrusted to you [that is, the good news about salvation through personal faith in Christ Jesus], through [the help of] the Holy Spirit who dwells in us. (2 Tim. 1:14 AMP)

Paul calls the truth that has been entrusted to us "treasure," or in the original Greek, *kalos* (good) + *paratheke* (deposit). When Jesus saved us by living a sinless life, dying on the cross, and defeating death by rising again, He gave us access to the greatest treasure of all: the truth of the gospel. It is a "good deposit" He's placed within believers.

Unlike my son's worthless pocket "twe-sures," the gospel is a treasure that required great sacrifice. And with the help of the Holy Spirit, we've been charged to guard it. This involves maintaining its integrity, keeping a close watch on it, and protecting it at all costs.

My husband and I recently took a trip to London and saw the British Crown Jewels at the Tower of London. Extreme measures have been put into place to guard this treasure: not only is it in a literal fortress, but there are posted guards, cameras, sensors, and more guards. Every measure is in place to keep the jewels safe.

When was the last time you recognized the treasure you've been given and consequently put measures in place to guard it well?

When we abide in the Lord, delight in His goodness, and take time to dwell on the treasure we've been given, our perspectives change. We *want* to spend more time with Him. We *want* to share about the treasure we've been given. And we *want* to preserve the truth of who God is and what He's done for us.

> Day by day we sit at His feet, asking for help to guard the life-changing treasure we've been given.

Second Corinthians 4:7 says, "But we have this treasure in jars of clay, to show that the surpassing power belongs to God and not to us."

Alone, we are incapable of protecting and guarding this treasure well. We are simply frail, breakable, perishable "jars of clay," and yet, it's the task we've been entrusted with. The power belongs to God and the Holy Spirit dwells within to help us in this calling.

But this means we must draw near. Day by day we sit at His feet, abiding, delighting, and asking for help to guard the precious, invaluable, life-changing treasure we've been given.

BE HELD

When I was little, my dad's lap was my favorite place to be. There was something about being held by him that made everything else seem a little less "hard." He erased the pain of a scraped knee, provided comfort after I made my very first basket for the wrong basketball team (true story), and even reminded me of God's truth when my feelings were hurt. In his lap, I felt safe, cared for, and loved.

We have a heavenly Father who deeply desires to hold us. There's a phrase in Zephaniah 3:17 that says, "He will quiet you by his love." And I think it's this picture; drawing so near to God that we allow His deep love for us to quiet our spirits, whisper His truth, and offer peace and joy, no matter the circumstances around us.

Here are a few practical ways to allow the Lord to hold you each day:

JUST BE WITH THE LORD

Schedule even a few minutes of time in your day to sit before the Lord. No phone, no distractions (depending on your life stage, this may be a challenge!), and no plans. During this time, ask the Lord to speak to your heart, to have a sense of Him holding you, and to remind you of His nearness.

IDENTIFY YOUR "TURKISH DELIGHT"

Is there something in your life you are delighting in more than God? Your family? Your job? Your "me" time? Admit this to the Lord, take some time to repent, and ask God to help you delight in Him instead.

TREASURE THE TREASURE

Recognize and value the "good deposit" you've been given in Christ. View the gospel as a treasure and set practical measures in place like clinging to the Word and sharing it frequently in an effort to guard it well.

There is nowhere better than the arms of Jesus. Don't miss the opportunity to day by day abide in Him.

QUESTIONS FOR REFLECTION

1. *Do you struggle to abide with Christ throughout your day? Is there anything that the Lord needs to prune in my life so I can build intimacy with Him?*

2. *What are some things you tend to delight in other than God? What can you do to lay these things aside?*

3. *What are some measures you can put into place to guard the treasure of the gospel well?*

VERSE TO MEMORIZE

"Abide in me, and I in you. As the branch cannot bear fruit by itself, unless it abides in the vine, neither can you, unless you abide in me."

—JOHN 15:4

CHAPTER SEVEN

LORD, I WANT TO BE MORE LIKE YOU

Discipline yourself for the purpose of godliness.

1 TIMOTHY 4:7 (NASB)

Some of my earliest memories are about being at church. Growing up, if the church doors were open, there was a good chance my family was there. My parents led small groups, helped in the children's ministry, served on committees, participated in mission trips, organized outreach projects, and more. As they attended and served, they brought me and my siblings along, teaching us to serve alongside them.

One of their favorite stories to tell happened when I couldn't have been much older than two or three. Each Sunday my parents would give us a coin to drop in the offering plate. However, this particular Sunday as they gave me my money, they told me the coin was to "give to Jesus."

And apparently, my eyes lit up and excitement grew as I eagerly asked, "Is He gonna be there today?!"

I think the reason this story is so loved and frequently told in my family is because those innocent words hold a lot of depth.

Is Jesus truly invited to be where we are, today? Have we paused in our busyness and schedules and serving (even in good things) long enough to look for His presence? Are our actions simply a result of going through the motions, or are they birthed out of a desire to be near and like the Lord?

It's not uncommon for us to jokingly look at each other and say, "Is He gonna be there today?!"

We've read how slowing down, creating margin, and surrendering our plans don't happen naturally. Instead, we must establish rhythms and practices designed to remind our hearts how to look for Jesus. These practices are also called spiritual disciplines.

Be honest though. What comes to mind when you hear the phrase "spiritual disciplines"? Do you instantly run in the opposite direction? Are you filled with shame or disappointment, feeling like you don't quite measure up? Do you think of them as nice ideas, but unattainable goals? Or do you beam with pride thinking you've checked enough of them off your list for the day?

The truth is, even if we've spent our whole lives in the church, we often don't fully understand what spiritual disciplines are, why we should put them into practice, and what they practically can look like in our lives. We have misconceptions, half-truths, and years of not-so-great experiences that shape our views.

However, what if we shifted our thinking, broke down what we thought we knew, and built it up with truths from God's Word? It starts with a humble heart and a simple prayer of, "Lord, I want to be more like You."

WHAT ARE SPIRITUAL DISCIPLINES?[23]

"Discipline yourself for the purpose of godliness" (1 Tim. 4:7 NASB).

Spiritual disciplines are deliberate practices done to turn our attention toward God. They are meant to help us center our lives around who Jesus is, what He's done for us, and the mission He's called us to fulfill (Matt. 28:18–20).

The Bible tells us in 2 Corinthians 3:18 that the Holy Spirit is transforming us into God's image. However, we have a part to play in obedience by putting into practice spiritual disciplines.

We must understand they are not a list of legalistic rules, not the ultimate goal of Christianity, nor necessary for salvation (Eph. 2:8–9). Instead, they are the means by which we pursue godliness.

We practice spiritual disciplines out of a deep love for Him and a desire to become more Christlike.

Here are some spiritual disciplines we see people practice in the Bible that you can implement yourself (we'll get into the details of some of these shortly, but I'll list Scripture references if you want to unpack any of these yourself):[24]

Spend time in the Word: Psalm 119:105, 2 Timothy 3:16

Pray: Philippians 4:6, Hebrews 4:16

Fellowship with other believers: Acts 2:42, Hebrews 10:24–25

Meditate on truths found in God's Word: Isaiah 26:3

Confess your sins to God: Proverbs 28:13, 1 John 1:9

Fast from food and/or other pleasures: Isaiah 58, Matthew 6:16–18

Serve others: Colossians 3:23–24

Spend time alone (solitude): Luke 5:16

Worship corporately and/or individually: 1 Chronicles 16:29

Observe the Sabbath: Leviticus 23:3, Mark 2:27–28

Give generously: Luke 12:33–34, 1 John 3:17

WHY SHOULD WE PRACTICE SPIRITUAL DISCIPLINES?

Remember how I was always at church growing up? I was also the child who would always have my verse memorized, my tithe in my pocket, and my Bible in hand when I showed up to Sunday school. I was determined to fill my sticker chart by completing these tasks. While these were good things and great practices to establish early, my heart was far more focused on the sticker chart than the God my memory verse was about.

God doesn't have a sticker chart with our names on it. We practice spiritual disciplines out of a deep love for Him and a growing desire to become Christlike.

In *Rest & War*, Ben Stuart puts it like this: "Any discipline we practice is a way to express and deepen our devotion to the Almighty."[25]

We don't only practice spiritual disciplines to deepen our devotion, but we practice spiritual disciplines to fight against our flesh. Disciplines require effort, attention, and a commitment that goes beyond how we feel.

In Romans 7:18 Paul writes, "For I know that nothing good dwells in me, that is, in my flesh. For I have the desire to do what is right, but not the ability to carry it out."

We don't have the ability to be Christlike on our own, but with the Spirit in us and our commitment to discipline ourselves, we do have the ability to take steps toward godliness.

HOW CAN WE PRACTICALLY IMPLEMENT SPIRITUAL DISCIPLINES?

All of this sounds good, but how can we do this when our days are busy, our free time is limited, and our spiritual life seems to fluctuate?

To oversimplify, you just do it: day by day, little by little.

Set aside ten minutes, then fifteen, then thirty to pursue the things of God. Use natural pauses and downtimes in your day (e.g., early mornings, daily commutes, lunch breaks, time when kids are napping or resting) to focus on a single spiritual discipline. Give up little things like phone time, TV time, or social media to make space. Then, when the space is created, use it purposefully.

Do you want to be more like Christ? If so, you will need to develop a lifestyle of setting your heart toward the Lord and your mind toward spiritual disciplines.

Let's take a deeper look at a few spiritual disciplines designed to help us slow down and join God in the work He is doing.

Spend Daily Time in the Word

The truth is, apart from Christ, we are sinful and as the old hymn says, "prone to wander . . . prone to leave the God I love."[26] Knowing this, daily time in the Word should not and cannot be optional . . . even if we have full schedules.

If we rightly posture our hearts, God can use our time in the Word to teach, reprove, correct, and train our hearts (2 Tim. 3:16). Because we are quick to forget, the time we spent yesterday is not sufficient for today. Our hearts need to daily draw near.

The Israelites learned a similar lesson in Exodus 16.

After they left Egypt, the Israelites found themselves wandering in the desert, hungry, complaining, and wrongly wishing to return

We must depend daily on the Lord to provide through His Word and faithfully obey the commands we receive.

to bondage. However, the Lord heard their grumbling and decided to provide daily nourishment for His people (v. 12).

Each morning manna from heaven appeared on the ground for the people to gather. The only requirement was that they only gather what they needed for each day (with the exception of a double portion the day before the Sabbath). The Lord wanted His people to daily depend on Him.

If the people gathered too much, the manna stank and bred worms. If they didn't gather enough for the Sabbath, none was given and they went hungry. Both dependence and obedience were required.

The same is required of us. We must depend daily on the Lord to provide through His Word and faithfully obey the commands we receive.[27]

There's no formula to this. Some people prefer a Bible reading plan and some prefer to walk through a specific book of the Bible self-paced. Some can spend time alone reading the Word in the morning, and some focus better in the evenings. I even have mom friends who know the quietest time they have is in the car and they listen to Scripture there. The important part is spending intentional time allowing the Word of God to feed your soul.

We own a giant ninety-pound white lab named Oakley and to say she loves to chew would be an understatement. She's almost ten now, but from the time she was a puppy, she's destroyed almost anything she can, especially if it's leather. You'd think I'd learn to keep things away from her, but over the years she's chewed up more than six leatherbound Bibles. It's heartbreaking and frustrating at the moment, but it does force me to buy a new Bible and start journaling fresh in each one. However, Dustin and I like to joke that she's just taking the whole "feasting on the Word of God" and "daily bread" thing literally.

You don't need to eat your Bible, but you do need to read it daily. It's not a chore, it's an opportunity to draw near to your Maker. Let His words comfort, sustain, encourage, and equip you to take part in His purposes each day.

Time in the Word isn't the only discipline we need to put into practice though.

Keep in Constant Communication[28]

Have you ever watched a toddler pray? If so, you may have seen the way they scrunch up their face, determined to keep their eyes closed. Or the way they wiggle, attempting to keep their hands in their lap and their head down. Or the way they get so excited once the prayer's over, knowing they made it through.

Does your prayer life ever look a little like a toddler's? Squirmy, forced, and more about completion than the process?

While we're in the trenches of day-to-day living, prayer (like most aspects of our lives) often feels all over the place. However, Scripture is full of truth and examples of what a healthy prayer life looks like no matter what life season we're in. It starts in the beginning.

In the garden, Adam and Eve had complete and tangible access to God. They spoke to Him and He heard and answered audibly (Gen. 2–3). But when they disobeyed the Lord and listened to the voice of the serpent, sin entered and as a result, they were driven out of the garden (Gen. 3:23–24). The voice they listened to mattered.

However, God in His goodness didn't cut off communication. Prayer is the means we have to continue speaking to and hearing from the Lord. Because of Jesus and His sacrifice on the cross, we still have complete access to the Father through the Spirit (Eph. 2:18). Hallelujah!

But how do we practically do that? How do we access the Father when the work project doesn't go well and the toddler is throwing a tantrum because you put her milk in the wrong sippy cup and you accidentally burn the cookies you were making for a neighbor?

God's Word is full of practical instruction. Among other things, He

Gave us an example of how to pray: Matthew 6:9–13

Encouraged us to pray about everything: Philippians 4:6–7

Promised He would hear us: 1 John 5:14

Told us prayer is powerful and effective: James 5:13–18

Prayer isn't about sitting still with our heads bowed and eyes closed (though it might be in the moment) or following a formula (though He may give you one to help you stay on track). It's about meeting with a loving and gracious Father who desires a relationship with us.

In the craziness of life, let's ask and anticipate He will meet us in the margins. Let's discipline ourselves to create structured times of prayer, and ask Him to teach us in the chaos, praying spontaneously as we go.

Spend Time Alone

Another lesser-discussed spiritual discipline is solitude. As we work to slow down and surrender our plans to the Lord, this one is important.

Solitude is the practice of getting away from everything and everyone that pulls at our attention in order to fully focus on the Lord. It's creating margin, silencing the noise, and asking God to meet us in the quiet (sounds kind of like a consistent theme in this book, right?!).

We see over and over in Scripture how Jesus "would withdraw to desolate places and pray" (Luke 5:16b).

One of the first times I practiced this discipline, I realized quickly how foreign this concept is. We live in a time where even when we are by ourselves, we aren't very often alone. Our phones tether us to others. Without my phone, I almost felt

The discipline of solitude has a way of magnifying the other disciplines.

lost and as though I didn't quite know what to do. But here's what God showed me: when we are faithful to remove distractions, He is faithful to multiply our efforts.

The discipline of solitude has a way of magnifying the other disciplines: prayer felt less rushed and more intimate, time in the Word felt more refreshing, and my mind felt sharper as I meditated without distraction.

You don't have to hike ten miles into the woods by yourself to practice solitude, and you don't even have to find complete silence, but you do have to set aside time and make a plan. It won't happen organically.

Here are a few practical ideas on how to practice solitude when your current life-stage makes it feel impossible:

> Get creative with location. Your car in the school pick-up line, the backyard, or even the bathroom (I'm getting vulnerable here, haha) can be places for solitude.

> Literally sneak away. I've backed out of a room as quietly as possible when the kids were playing happily just to get a few minutes of solitude in my closet.

> Set boundaries with your phone. Commit to leaving it in the other room to charge or turning it off at certain points so your solitude won't be interrupted by technology.

Be honest with others around you about your need for solitude. Ask your spouse, friend, or family member if they'd be willing to give up an evening to watch kids or take over your responsibilities so you can get away to be with the Lord.

Be willing to sacrifice. You may need to give up sleep and go to bed late, wake up in the night, or wake up early to have solitude. You may need to say no to a night out with friends or another activity if it means you can get away. Remember, rarely does solitude happen organically.

Add it to the calendar. There will always be excuses and reasons and tasks fighting to draw us away from intimate time with the Lord. Set aside time and do what it takes to protect it. It's worth it!

There's one more discipline I want to break down in light of living a life surrendered to God's purposes.

Meet Together

While we do need to create times of solitude, the other side of the coin is true, too: We need to prioritize getting together with other believers. This means slowing down enough to put into practice the disciplines of fellowship, service, and corporate worship.[29]

As we learn about the early church through Scripture, we see how God designed for us to purposefully get together. Take a look at this encouragement from Hebrews:

> And let us consider how to stir up one another to love and good works, not neglecting to meet together, as is the habit of some, but encouraging one another, and all the more as you see the Day drawing near. (Heb. 10:24–25)

Meeting together with a local body of believers is one of the most beautiful gifts God has given us on this side of eternity. We need each other!

A few years ago on a mission trip to Paris, I had the opportunity to worship with a small group of local believers there made up of multiple ethnicities and languages. In fact, the sermon was translated four times, and the worship leader even rotated the language songs were sung in. Even though this community had to work hard to overcome language and cultural barriers, the love they had for each other was evident. It centered around their unity in Christ. Unlike most of us here in America, when each member of this congregation left church that morning, they knew they might not encounter another believer until the following Sunday. This time was more than "just going to church." This was the encouragement they needed to keep fighting the good fight, to step out into a lost world knowing they're not alone, to be strengthened for the work ahead.

Like all spiritual disciplines though, meeting together and willingly investing in others is a choice.

Have you noticed how creating "community" has been somewhat of a hot topic lately? We hear phrases like "doing life with each other" or the warning "not to live life alone" thrown around frequently. Couple this with social media photos of groups sitting around discussing theology over perfectly brewed coffee, and it's easy to look at our community and think it's not quite measuring up.

So, what should biblical community truly look like?

The Oxford dictionary defines community as "a feeling of fellowship with others, as a result of sharing common attitudes, interests, and goals."[30] And in the case of biblical community, those shared interests and goals are Jesus and His mission of making disciples (Matt. 28:18–20).

In Romans 15, Paul explains living in biblical community looks a lot like setting aside your own desires to meet the needs of others—just like Jesus did. He then writes:

"Now may the God who gives perseverance and encouragement grant you to be of the same mind with one another, according to Christ Jesus, so that with one purpose and one voice you may glorify the God and Father of our Lord Jesus Christ. Therefore, accept one another, just as Christ also accepted us, for the glory of God" (Rom. 15:5–7 NASB).

This passage shows us three principles of biblical community:

Members of a community strive to be of the same mind

This is a call for unity, not uniformity. In Christ, we have the same mission, but we need each other to complete it (1 Cor. 12). Use the gifts you've been given to serve within your community and encourage others to do the same.

The purpose of community is to glorify God

Community exists not solely for our own benefit (though we do benefit from it) but for the purpose of glorifying God. When we deny ourselves and serve others, we are living displays of the gospel. Encouraging, admonishing, and loving others is a way to bring glory to Him.

Community welcomes others in

Biblical communities are not exclusive. Yes, we are to pursue deep, meaningful, long-term relationships, but we are also called to welcome new brothers and sisters in. Accept each other, invite new friends into your community, and consider others before yourself.

When seasons of hardship and grief hit—we need each other.

When seasons of comfort and joy flourish—we need each other. Community is life-giving, good, and honoring to God.

What does your community look like? Are you pursuing unity and staying on mission? As you build community, is it your heart's desire to give the glory to God? Do you invite others to join you?

All of this requires slowing down. When we are too busy, we have the potential to not only miss the needs of others, but also our need for relationship with them. If your schedule is so packed that it prohibits meeting together, it may be an indication to lay some things aside and discipline yourself to invest in community. This doesn't mean you should say yes to every Bible study and church event possible, but it does mean you make investing in community a priority.

When we are too busy, we have the potential to not only miss the needs of others, but also our need for relationship with them.

MORE LIKE JESUS

We started this chapter with the simple prayer, "Lord, I want to be more like You." I love how this postures our hearts to prioritize God and His purposes. But the overflow of our hearts is action.

This chapter only skims the surface of spiritual disciplines (we didn't even cover them all), but here are a few good places to start:

ASK, "IS HE GONNA BE THERE TODAY?"

Are you slowing down enough to look for God at work around you? Start making it a practice to pause, pray, and ask God to open your eyes. Transitions from one part of your day to the next are the perfect opportunity for this (e.g., driving from home to work, pausing for your lunch break, right before your child wakes up from his nap, before dinner, etc.).

SET ASIDE TEN MINUTES TO FOCUS ON A SPIRITUAL DISCIPLINE

It's wise to start small. Keep in mind some disciplines "add to" and others "abstain." Ask God what area of your life needs to be more disciplined and focus on that first. Schedule this time out each day so it becomes a natural rhythm and priority for you.

FEAST ON THE WORD

Ask God to increase your hunger for Scripture. Start changing your view of Bible reading from something to check off the list to something you need, desire, and want above almost everything else.

EVALUATE YOUR BIBLICAL COMMUNITY

And start with yourself. Are you pursuing unity, glorifying God, and welcoming others? Then look for something you could do practically to show others in your community the love of God. Could you take them a meal, invite them over, watch their kids, help them with yard work, something else? Make this a priority this week.

When we view spiritual disciplines through the lens of becoming Christlike, we start to fall in love with the practice. Our days will slow, our eyes will shift to eternity, and we will start prioritizing God's purposes over our plans.

QUESTIONS FOR REFLECTION

1. *What do you think of when you hear the word "spiritual disciplines"? Does your view need to change based on what you've learned in this chapter?*

2. *Which spiritual discipline is a struggle for you? What can you do to start to make this more of a priority in your life?*

3. *How can you rearrange your schedule to prioritize spiritual disciplines?*

VERSE TO MEMORIZE

Discipline yourself for the purpose of godliness.

—1 TIMOTHY 4:7 (NASB)

CHAPTER EIGHT

WHAT ABOUT WORK?

So, whether you eat or drink, or whatever you do,
do all to the glory of God.

1 CORINTHIANS 10:31

As his baby blue eyes welled with tears, my son's voice quivered as he quietly asked, "Why does Daddy have to go to work?" After a week of vacation spent together on the beach, Monday morning was hitting us hard and frankly, it wasn't just my son who was upset. I looked around and saw the suitcases filled with dirty clothes, the empty refrigerator, and the mile-long list of unopened emails and felt a lot like my son: upset at the idea of work.

However, in those few overwhelming moments, my husband gently reminded both me and my son of the eternal value of work. He spoke of the financial realities that had made our vacation possible. He explained how working as a team and achieving goals is exciting and rewarding. And most importantly, he reminded us of the role he (and we) have to live on mission in our workplaces.

His urging didn't necessarily change the reality or quantity of work I had to do that day, and it didn't instantaneously dry my son's tears, but it reminded me that work, like rest, is of and for the Lord. It's our job to both find the balance and remain on mission.

Up until this point, we've looked at creating margin and living unhurried, and the truth is, we love the idea of slowing down. We want to sip coffee on the back porch dreamily staring out at the lake or sit on the beach with a good book and no agenda. However, there's this little (big) part of life called work. How can we slow down and create margin when we have meetings at ten, two, and four? Or when work in the home is literally never-ending?

In short, we must have a right understanding of work, rest, and an inner sense of unhurriedness.

WHY DO WE WORK?

Have you heard of the "Sunday Scaries"?

According to the podcast by this name, "the Sunday Scaries are the anxiety that sets in on Sunday nights with the impending return to the office, school, or work."[31]

I distinctly remember being at Sunday night church in middle school and dreading the ending song. It wasn't because I didn't want to sing anymore, it was because I knew the minute it was over, we would go home, and I'd have to get ready for school the next day. I don't know what middle school was like for you, but if it was anything like my experience, I wouldn't exactly call it the glory days. Girls were mean, I was far from confident, and I disliked much of the work. The Sunday Scaries hit me hard.

In our fast-paced society, having anxiety about work is so common, we've given it a name. And the truth is, we often speak of work as a negative thing. It's synonymous with hardship, toil, striving, and exhaustion. But the reality is this: Work was God's design for us from the beginning.

Shortly after God made Adam, Genesis 2 tells us: "The LORD God took the man and put him in the Garden of Eden to **work it** and **take care of it**" (Gen. 2:15 NIV).

It's important to realize this took place before the fall recorded in Genesis 3. At this point, sin hadn't entered the world, and Adam and Eve dwelled with God in the garden. Things were as they should be. And yet, work was involved.

This alone should change our view of work. Work was never intended to be God's punishment for us, and we'll look at how the curse changed that shortly. Instead, work was designed to give us purpose and fulfillment alongside our Creator. Can you imagine what Adam's work was like? As he took care of the garden where God had placed him, all was as it should be. He toiled not laboriously, but gladly, knowing the work He did was an act of honor and obedience toward God.

However, the fall and resulting curse of sin changed the reality of work. Take a look at Genesis 3:17b–19:

> "Because you have listened to the voice of your wife
>> and have eaten of the tree
> of which I commanded you,
>> 'You shall not eat of it,'
> cursed is the ground because of you;
>> **in pain** you shall eat of it all the days of your life;
> thorns and thistles it shall bring forth for you;
>> and you shall eat the plants of the field.
> **By the sweat of your face**
>> you shall eat bread,
> till you return to the ground,
>> for out of it you were taken;
> for you are dust,
>> and to dust you shall return."

Before the fall, work was pleasant. After the fall, work became hard, toilsome, and laborious. Now Adam was to work as before, but things wouldn't go his way. The ground would produce thorns and only by his sweat would he be able to provide for his family.

And unfortunately, this is our reality, too. We are to work, but it won't always be easy.

For us to have a right understanding of work, we must take it a step further, because, unlike Adam, we live in a post-messianic world. Jesus has come, set us free from sin, and given us a new mission: to love God and love others, even through our work.

The church at Colossae had similar questions about the value of work, so in Paul's letter, he addressed work in relation to Christian households. He wrote: "Whatever you do, work heartily, as for the Lord and not for men, knowing that from the Lord you will receive the inheritance as your reward. You are serving the Lord Christ" (Col. 3:23–24).

How do we serve Jesus as we wait for His return? We work heartily.

I love how Paul encompasses all kinds of work in his statement "whatever you do." Work looks different for all of us. You may be sitting on campus preparing for a test or in the middle of your twelve-hour shift at the hospital or looking around your house seeing numerous tasks that need to be done—it's all work. It's not necessarily easy or fun or even rewarding (financially or otherwise), but it is how we serve Jesus as we wait for His return.

But what if you don't? What if you choose not to do the work God has entrusted to you, whatever and wherever that might be? Does it really affect your relationship with the Lord and with others?

Solomon, the wisest man to ever live, thought so:

> Go to the ant, O sluggard;
> consider her ways, and be wise.

Without having any chief,
    officer, or ruler,
she prepares her bread in summer
    and gathers her food in harvest.
How long will you lie there, O sluggard?
    When will you arise from your sleep?
A little sleep, a little slumber,
    a little folding of the hands to rest,
and poverty will come upon you like a robber,
    and want like an armed man. (Prov. 6:6–11)

As the mom of three young boys and a sweet baby girl following in their footsteps, I spend my fair share of time looking at and learning about all kinds of bugs. There's rarely a day that passes where I'm not answering questions about insects. And while I still choose to keep my distance from the majority of creepy-crawly things, I've also learned just how impressive they can be.

Nobody tells the ants to gather food and prepare for winter, and yet they do. Nobody encourages them to work together or get started early or work long hours, but they do. As a result, they have the food they need to survive.

> **Work is not income-driven but purpose-driven. What is God calling you to do?**

Rest, margin, and a slower pace of life do not give us permission to become sluggards. Sluggards fail to honor God and instead slip into full dependence on others.

To go back to the question above, yes, failing to do the work God has called us to affects our relationship with both God and others. As a reminder and point of clarity, work is not income-driven but purpose-driven. What is God calling you to do? How can you fulfill the mission He's set before you? This is the work that needs to be done. And once the work is done for the hour or day or week, we rest.

WHY DO WE REST?

If you were to ask any one of my sons when they were toddlers why we rest, they would show off their obviously gigantic muscles and tell you, "So God can grow me big and strong!" And, in many ways, they would be right. As we rest, God not only allows our physical bodies relief and time to recover and restore, but He also rejuvenates us spiritually, too.

Our rest strengthens and equips us for times of work.

The evidence is most clearly seen in the commandment of the Sabbath. As Moses went up Mount Sinai to meet with God, this is what he received as the fourth commandment:

> "Remember the Sabbath day, to keep it holy. Six days you shall labor, and do all your work, but the seventh day is a Sabbath to the LORD your God. On it you shall not do any work, you, or your son, or your daughter, your male servant, or your female servant, or your livestock, or the sojourner who is within your gates. For in six days the LORD made heaven and earth, the sea, and all that is in them, and rested on the seventh day. Therefore the LORD blessed the Sabbath day and made it holy." (Ex. 20:8–11)

This commandment was given to a people who were used to work. As slaves in Egypt, the Israelites were nearly crushed by the amount of toil and labor forced upon them. However, as they found themselves free, and in the desert, this is one of the ten commandments given to them.

A Sabbath day, or a day of rest, is simply time dedicated to the Lord. It's holy, set apart, distinct, consecrated, so we can realign our hearts and minds with His. Even though we no longer live under the old covenant, rest is wise and a big deal in God's eyes.

Notice a few things about this commandment:

Rest on this day helps keep it holy.

The Lord rested, so we rest.

A day of rest is blessed by the Lord.

Did the Lord need to rest after creation? Probably not . . . He's God. But do we need to rest? Yes! We need to depend on Him to provide for us even as we rest, and we need to experience the blessings rest brings.

So if we acknowledge rest is needed, we also need to ask what rest looks like. Does this mean one day a week we stay in bed and stare at the wall? No, although I must admit there are some days this seems more appealing than others. It means we create purposeful margin and ask God to meet us there.

Purposeful Margin

Purposeful margin really is what it sounds like: it's a setting aside of time for the Lord. Now, what the Lord chooses to do with this time is up to His calling and our obedience.

Soon after the Lord started teaching me about slowing down, I sensed His call to lay aside time and create this purposeful margin. As someone who has to plan to not have a plan, this was easier said than done. However, one of the first few times I determined to leave a day open for the Lord's plans, He was so good to show me why.

My morning started similar to every other day with coffee and caring for littles. Then, if you need further evidence of the way our hurried lives affect others, I quickly saw it as my son promptly asked,

"What are we going to do today? Are we going somewhere or is some-one coming over?" However, instead of listing off chores, errands, and plans like normal, I simply answered, "I don't know, we are going to do whatever God asks us to," not even knowing myself what that meant.

I turned on worship music, spent some time in the Word, and felt burdened to pray for a friend who doesn't have a relationship with Jesus. Less than half an hour later, I glanced at my phone only to see a text from that same friend asking us if we wanted to head to a nearby neighborhood park. Since we didn't have existing plans, my response was an easy yes.

The playdate at the park was typical with countless interruptions from toddlers demanding to be pushed on the swings or caught at the bottom of the slide, but it was atypical in the sense that I knew the Lord, not me, had planned this time. My focus was on Him and my spirit was in tune with His promptings. Doors opened for gospel conversations, and even though my friend didn't surrender her life to Jesus that day, she heard the truth and asked questions.

After the park, we headed home to more of an empty but willing agenda, and this is going to sound way less exciting than sharing the gospel, but I lay down on the couch and took a nap.

Yep, crazy, I know!

However, if you know me, you also know this in and of itself is evidence of the Lord's working. I've never been a napper. Instead, I can always identify something else that needs to be done.

But on this day, the nap came easily. There was no guilt or feeling of laziness, no other responsibilities on my mind, no interruptions from children or work, just a sweet gift of rest from the Lord.

That's the thing about purposeful margin: it's not a formula or plan or series of events, it's a willingness to go if the Lord says to go and stay if the Lord says to stay. And it's this surrender of our day that creates a restful and dependent spirit.

Have you ever taken time to create purposeful margin? If so, how did you see the Lord work?

Here's my challenge to you: set aside time (whether it's a day or simply a few unaccounted-for hours) and surrender it to the Lord. During that time, pray, rest, get in the Word, intercede for others, and ask God to align your plans with His. Be willing to follow, surrender, and obey when prompted.

Needed Rest

As we look at work and rest, there's one more side to rest we shouldn't ignore: needed rest. This rest is different from purposeful margin in that it's not time we set aside, it's time we need in order to be prepared to work again. This includes sleep at the end of each day, time in recovery after sickness, relief when we are burdened, and freedom from the striving of the world.

In Matthew 11:28–30, we encounter one of the most popular verses of Scripture about rest:

> "Come to me, all who labor and are heavy laden, and I will give you rest. Take my yoke upon you, and learn from me, for I am gentle and lowly in heart, and you will find rest for your souls. For my yoke is easy, and my burden is light."

Yes, this is a verse about rest (specifically needed rest), but it's more than that. This passage is an invitation to turn away from sin and a works-based religion to enter into a relationship with Jesus. At the heart, it's a verse about the character of Jesus.

He gives us rest from laboring and trying to be what the world says we should be—successful, happy, powerful—and instead offers this salvation and freedom from striving. He knows, because He faced it all, and in Him we find rest.

Take a minute to think about the implications. He knows He's asked us to go and make disciples, and He knows it's not going to be easy (take a look at some of the trials of the disciples if you aren't sure), but He doesn't leave us there. He offers to walk with us, to take the troubles upon Himself, and to give rest.

But how do we engage in needed rest and walk in the freedom He offers? Look at the verse again:

> Come to Jesus—First and foremost in salvation, and then regularly spending time with Him through the Word and prayer.
>
> Take My yoke upon you—His ways and His will are easier to surrender to as we live by faith with our eyes on eternity.
>
> Learn from Me—Live as His disciple or follower.

This needed rest is what gives us the energy daily to accomplish what God desires. The Christian life is not one of striving, it's one of surrender. His yoke is easy and His burden is light.

A WARNING AGAINST IDLENESS

Some years ago, the idea of "cardboard testimonies" became popular in the Christian world. The practice was simple: you would write a word or phrase that described your life before Christ on one side of the cardboard, and then flip it over and write a word or phrase that described your life after Christ. For example, you might write "slave to perfection" on one side and "free in Christ" on the other.

I distinctly remember my high school youth group excitedly hopping on the trend. We all took some time to pray and think about what we would write, and then during a Wednesday night service, we took turns standing on the stage to show one side of our cardboard and then the other. Many of my friends wrote about insecurities or fears they had dealt with, but mine said something like this: "marked by idleness" to "actively living on mission."

I decided to follow Jesus when I was six years old, but by the time I was a teenager, I had become content in spiritual stagnation. My spiritual life was idle, my work/school life was idle, and even relationships in my life had become idle. It was during this cardboard testimony exercise the Lord revealed to me the sin of my idle living and called me to return to my mission of making disciples.

In our lives, idleness looks like laziness, slothfulness, and even an aversion to work. It's the same picture of a car idling: the engine is running, but the car isn't going anywhere.

As we've learned about creating margin and living unhurried, we must remember that neither purposeful margin nor needed rest is an excuse for idleness. Scripture warns us of the dangers.

The church body in Thessalonica received this warning from Paul in 2 Thessalonians 3:6–15. Paul goes so far as to tell them to "keep away from any brother who is walking in idleness" (v. 6) because those who walk in idleness are "not busy at work, but busybodies" (v. 11). Yikes!

Have you ever met someone you would describe as a busybody? Generally, they aren't very pleasant to be around. The dictionary defines a busybody as "an officious or inquisitive person."[32] Maybe this is the neighbor who is always spreading gossip or offering unwanted advice, or maybe this is someone you know who always manages to take and never give.

As believers, Paul calls us to be the opposite. We are to be faithful workers. In 2 Thessalonians 3:13 (NASB), he writes this: "But as for you, brothers and sisters, do not grow weary of doing good."

Did you catch that? To combat idleness, we work. And we don't work aimlessly, we work for the good of others and the glory of God. We stay on mission.

Have you confused your need for rest with idleness? Has your creation of margin actually turned into laziness?

Here are a few indicators of idleness to be wary of:

You are constantly relying on the provisions and goodwill of others. (Constantly being the keyword here. This is not talking about seasons when this is needed.)

You aren't working in a job, in your home, or in your community.

You spend more time concerned about other people's business than your own.

Other people could describe you as a busybody.

As you reflect on your day/week/month, you can't describe anything you have accomplished for Christ.

You haven't shared the gospel with anyone recently.

You feel purposeless and like your life doesn't have meaning.

You aren't living on mission.

If any of these describe you, it may be time to turn away from idleness and work for the glory of God. And why must we deal with idleness? So we don't become burdensome and hinder our witnesses.

Jesus came to give us abundant life (John 10:10). Don't waste yours by remaining idle.

BALANCING IT ALL

So what does it look like practically to live out these truths? Can we truly find the balance between rest and work? And most importantly, how do we do it in a way that honors God?

In short, we live Spirit-led lives.

As soon as we make the decision to follow Jesus, we gain the Holy Spirit. Scripture helps us understand how to know Him and follow His promptings. Because of this, I want to take a break from our typical end-of-chapter practicality tips, and instead take them straight from Scripture.

If we want to live Spirit-led lives, we can:

ASK THE FATHER

"If you then, who are evil, know how to give good gifts to your children, how much more will the heavenly Father give the Holy Spirit to those who ask him!" (Luke 11:13).

SET OUR MIND ON THE SPIRIT'S DESIRES

"Those who live according to the flesh have their minds set on what the flesh desires; but those who live in accordance with the Spirit have their minds set on what the Spirit desires. The mind governed by the flesh is death, but the mind governed by the Spirit is life and peace" (Rom. 8:5–6 NIV).

BEAR THE SPIRIT'S FRUITS AND KEEP IN STEP WITH HIM

"But the fruit of the Spirit is love, joy, peace, forbearance, kindness, goodness, faithfulness, gentleness and self-control. Against such things there is no law. Those who belong to Christ Jesus have crucified the flesh with its passions and desires. Since we live by the Spirit, let us keep in step with the Spirit" (Gal. 5:22–25 NIV).

Make Sure We Don't Quench or Grieve Him

"Do not quench the Spirit" (1 Thess. 5:19).

"And do not grieve the Holy Spirit of God, by whom you were sealed for the day of redemption" (Eph. 4:30).

As we begin to do these things and follow the Spirit's promptings, we will learn how to better balance rest and work. This looks different for each one of us and may even look different as we enter different life seasons.

For example, the work that may have taken you an hour in your twenties may take you half a day in your sixties. There is grace in this. And the sleep you require as a teenager may be cut in half in the days you spend raising little ones. There is grace in this, too.

First Corinthians 10:31 reminds us: "So, whether you eat or drink, or whatever you do, do all to the glory of God."

Don't miss this. If you rest, do it for the glory of God. If you work, do it for the glory of God. This is a life well lived.

QUESTIONS FOR REFLECTION

1. *What does your work life look like? Is it honoring to God?*

2. *Have you ever intentionally created purposeful margin? If so, how did you see God use that time?*

3. *Would you describe any area of your life as idle? What is it, and how can you instead live mission-minded?*

VERSE TO MEMORIZE

So, whether you eat or drink, or whatever you do, do all to the glory of God.

—1 CORINTHIANS 10:31

CHAPTER NINE

USING YOUR GIFTS

As each has received a gift, use it to serve one another,
as good stewards of God's varied grace.

1 PETER 4:10

For several years now, I've served on the leadership team at church for women's ministry.

Oddly enough, it started alongside this call from the Lord to write. On a not-quite-fall-yet September day after a chaotic morning dropping my kids off at Mother's Day Out, I tentatively walked into our former women's minister's office to share a little about what God was doing in my life.

As God does, He had already been working on her heart, too, placing a desire in her to expand our women's ministry's blog and social media impact. One thing led to another, doors started opening, and it wasn't long before I was eagerly writing and serving on this team. I've learned a lot through the years, not just about women's ministry, but about what serving the church and working alongside others could and should look like.

Shortly after I started serving on the women's ministry team, we decided to host a women's potluck. Our church is multigenerational, and while "cooking" isn't listed in Scripture as a spiritual gift, I fully believe there are some women in our church who have a God-given gift to prepare incredible food and have been serving in this way for over fifty years. I'm not the best chef myself but, wanting to contribute, I brought an easy Pinterest dip and set it out along with a bag of store-bought tortilla chips on the table next to their delicacies.

As the evening went on, I watched as women of all life stages filtered in, bringing different types of foods, and then sitting alongside one another to eat and enjoy. As I watched, I couldn't help but realize what an amazing picture of the church this was.

You bring something. I bring something. We partake together.

We spent a whole chapter looking at the value of work, but two critical pieces we can't overlook and need to unpack are the spiritual gifts we've been given, and the roles God has asked us to fulfill.

If every woman at the potluck had brought the exact same food, it would've ended up being pretty boring, and I'm almost certain we would've all been sick of that food by the end of it. The potluck would have also turned out for the worse if I had been assigned to prepare the technical delicacy while my dear friend who loves to cook had been asked to bring the bag of chips. Instead, it was important we all "stayed in our lane" and did what we knew we could and should do well.

So how do we live this out? And what does it have to do with slowing down and keeping God's purposes at the forefront of our minds? Plus, how are we even supposed to know what our gifts are and what our role is?

As always, Scripture is where we turn when these types of questions arise.

WHAT ARE SPIRITUAL GIFTS?

If you've been in the church for very long at all, chances are you've heard the term "spiritual gifts." Maybe your pastor preached a sermon on one of the four main passages where spiritual gifts are discussed. Maybe you've heard people casually talking about how _____ is their spiritual gift. Or maybe, you've even been encouraged to take some sort of spiritual gifts assessment.

For years, I fell in all three of the above categories. I could even tell you the results of my assessment: primary gifts of shepherding, teaching, and knowledge, secondary gifts of wisdom and faith, and little to no giftings of music and mercy (I'm sure this isn't shocking if you know me at all).

But despite all of this, I think many believers have an incomplete—if not wrong—view of spiritual gifts. It would take a whole book to do a thorough deep dive, but I do want us to look at them through the lens of living unhurried and purposeful lives. Knowing what spiritual gifts are and identifying our spiritual gifts helps us know how to prioritize tasks and walk in obedience to the Lord. It also helps us know when to say no and allow others to step up to use their gifts.

So, what are spiritual gifts?

Paula Vawter, a wise Bible teacher, and dear mentor and friend, has studied spiritual gifts for three decades and compiled this definition that I love:[33]

> Spiritual gifts are a divine, supernatural ability, given by
> God at the time of salvation (which is when one receives the
> Holy Spirit). These spiritual gifts are revealed, developed,
> and matured over the course of the believer's lifetime, in
> accordance with God's timing and in conjunction with the

believer's desire and obedience to discover and develop their individual gifts. Spiritual gifts are given to every individual believer, without merit; enabling them to serve, to motivate, and to facilitate their service in the body of Christ. All to the glory of God!

I think it's also important to know that the Greek word used in 1 Corinthians 12, Romans 12, and 1 Peter 4 for "gifts" is *charisma*.[34] The root of this word is *charis*,[35] which means "grace." With only one semester of Greek in college, I'm far from a Greek scholar, but what I do know is these words in the original language mean each of our giftings comes from God. They are not anything we could achieve or obtain on our own; instead, they truly are gifts. As gifts, they are to be used for the building up of the body of Christ.

> **Talents typically impact the here and now while spiritual gifts have an impact from now into eternity.**

These are more than just natural talents or skills. You can look around and easily identify people who can do amazing things. There are incredible artists, athletes, scholars who have immense talents. But this doesn't necessarily mean they have or are using spiritual gifts.

Everyone has some sort of talent, but only believers possess the Holy Spirit. This means only believers have spiritual gifts. And unlike talents that may be used for entertainment or personal gain, spiritual gifts are to be used for the common good (1 Cor. 12:7), to serve one another (1 Peter 4:10), and for the equipping of the saints (Eph. 4:12–13). Talents typically impact the here and now while spiritual gifts have an impact from now into eternity.

Scripture does mention specific gifts, and while I'm not going to get into the details (but would strongly encourage you to study on your own at some point), I want you to see a list of the different giftings. They are found in Romans 12:3–13, 1 Corinthians 12, Ephesians 4:1–16, and 1 Peter 4:10–11 and include the following:

Administration	Knowledge
Apostleship	Leadership
Discernment	Mercy
Evangelism	Miracles
Exhortation	Music
Faith	Prophecy
Giving	Service
Healing	Shepherding
Helping	Speaking in tongues
Hospitality	Teaching
Interpretation of tongues	Wisdom
Intercession	

Here's what I pray you take away. As a believer, you have been given a gift or gifts from the Spirit, and not only is this amazing, but it is also freeing! These gifts mean you aren't supposed to do it all.

Look what Paul says in 1 Corinthians 12:14–20:

> For the body does not consist of one member but of many. If the foot should say, "Because I am not a hand, I do not belong to the body," that would not make it any less a part of the body. And if the ear should say, "Because I am not an eye, I do not belong to the body," that would not make it any less a part of the body. If the whole body were an eye, where would be the sense of hearing? If the whole body were an ear, where would be the sense of smell? But as it is, God arranged the members in the body, each one of them, as he chose. If

all were a single member, where would the body be? As it is, there are many parts, yet one body.

So often we become busy and overcommitted and stretched too thin because we're trying to be an eye when God has instead gifted us with hearing. Knowing and understanding our giftings frees us to be the ear and stop trying to be the eye too. God, in His sovereignty, has distributed gifts perfectly to accomplish His purposes. It's our job to creatively explore and ultimately embrace what we've been given and use it for His glory. God wants us to slow down, identify our gifts, and start asking Him how He wants us to use them for the building up of the body.

But how do we know what our spiritual gifts are?

IDENTIFYING MY SPIRITUAL GIFTS

For over ten years, my husband and I have directed various small groups at our church. We started directing a nearly/newlywed class, then a young marrieds class, then a parents of littles class, and now we love leading a parents of elementary kids class (haha, it's as though we just keep aging).

However, when we started serving in this way, my husband was fairly adamant we should simply direct or lead the class organizationally, not teach. Wanting to submit to his leadership, that's what we did at first. But, because I know him, I'd also seen how he had an amazing ability to explain things well to people and to guide them to deeper understanding.

Sure enough, as we started directing, times would come up when our teacher would be out and ask Dustin to teach. What started as a reluctant yes from him, turned into an easy yes, and then turned into an eager yes. As Dustin started to teach, he realized not only was he able, but he enjoyed it and was good at it (even if he won't admit it). He has the ability to understand, explain, and apply the Word of God in ways many others don't. Dustin has the spiritual gift of teaching.

Now, every other week, Dustin teaches. He spends hours in study and preparation and works hard to use this gift to communicate the truth of God's Word. So how did he know he had the gift of teaching? I think there are a few things that went into it: other people noticed it in him, he sought the Lord when opportunities came up, he realized it brought him enjoyment, and he saw how it drew others closer to the Lord.

So is this the only way to identify spiritual gifts? I don't think so. Here are a few things you can do.

Ask God

Right before Paul discusses spiritual gifts in Romans, he writes this in Romans 12:1–2 (NASB):

> I urge you, brothers and sisters, by the mercies of God, to present your bodies as a living and holy sacrifice, acceptable to God, which is your spiritual service of worship. And do not be conformed to this world, but be transformed by the renewing of your mind, so that you may prove what the will of God is, that which is good and acceptable and perfect.

If you want to know what your spiritual gifts are, offer yourself to God. Spend time in the Word. Seek Him in prayer. In this, you'll be able to discern what God's will is for your life and what gifts He's graciously given to you.

Ask Other, Mature Believers

Just as I knew Dustin had a unique ability to communicate biblical truths in easy-to-understand ways before he did, there may be people in your life who see things you might not be aware of yet. There is wisdom in seeking counsel. Ask those in your life who know you well and who walk with the Lord what gifts they see in you.

I would caution you in solely taking their word as truth though. Use discernment from the Lord and bring it all before Him. He is the authority. But He can and does use those around you.

Examine Yourself

Next, take some time to really look at your life. As you do, here are some good questions to ask:

> What are things people typically ask me to do?
>
> What are my spiritual strengths? What about spiritual weaknesses?
>
> What areas have I seen success in ministry?
>
> What areas of service and ministry am I drawn to the most?
>
> Where is God confirming my gift?
>
> What do I like doing in ministry? What things bring me joy?

Serving, no matter the capacity, likely won't be "fun" 100 percent of the time, but there is a deep, soul-satisfying joy that comes when you're serving using the gift(s) God has given you. Don't get stuck doing what you think you have to do or have always done, instead ask God to show you where you can use the gifts He has given you to serve the church.

It may be that you're using your gift without even knowing it. Honestly answering these questions may help to give you insight.

Take a Spiritual Gifts Assessment

Consider taking a spiritual gifts assessment. I mentioned this earlier in the chapter, and there are some really great (and free) ones out there. However, keep in mind these are tests developed by man in an attempt to identify spiritual things. This means they can help indicate what your spiritual gifts may be, but the Spirit is the only one who gives and reveals your gifts. Regard this as a tool and nothing more.

Knowing what your gift (or gifts) are is huge when it comes to slowing down and creating margin. This knowledge helps us know what to say yes to and what we could and should hand to someone else. But this knowledge also means we have a responsibility.

WHAT DO I DO WITH THE GIFTS I'VE BEEN GIVEN?

I love this simple illustration from Warren Wiersbe. He wrote:

> The thief says, "What's yours is mine—I'll take it!"
>
> The selfish man says, "What's mine is mine—I'll keep it!"
>
> But the Christian must say, "What's mine is a gift from God—I'll share it."[36]

How we use our gifts matters. They are to be shared with the body for the glory of God.

I think one of the reasons I love the 1 Corinthians 12 illustration about the body so much is that it's such an amazing picture of the way the church is supposed to function. Our gifts aren't meant to put us in competition with each other; instead, they are designed to help us complement one another—bringing unity, peace, and an effective witness to a very disunified world.

How are you using your gift? Have you turned a blind eye to needs in your local body you know you're equipped to fulfill? Are you serving in ways that don't allow you to use your gifts? If so, is there someone else better gifted to serve in that position?

You have been given your particular gifts for a purpose. Don't neglect them, hide behind them, covet other gifts, or use them to bring attention to yourself instead of God. Instead, take some time to surrender any way your gifts might not fit into your plan, and instead ask God how He wants you to use them to step into the role He's purposed for you.

WHAT IS MY ROLE?

In your current season of life, what would you say your job is? Your calling? Your role? Your purpose?

These questions are multifaceted and to be completely honest, more murky than I'd like. It's not always easy for us to define what it is we are supposed to do. To complicate it further, oftentimes what the world would demand of us is a far cry from what God asks of us.

As seasons of life change and we mature, our callings/ jobs/roles will change and develop with us.

As believers, we all have a united purpose in fulfilling the Great Commission to "go therefore and make disciples" (Matt. 28:19a). But we also have individual roles and tasks God assigns to each of us. I believe it's important for us to know and recognize what God is specifically asking of us so we will again know how to "stay in our lane."

We have been given specific roles for a unified purpose: to glorify God, build up the body, and make disciples. In the same way, we have different spiritual gifts, we also have different roles. Again, if we all did the same thing it would make for a pretty ineffective witness.

This doesn't only apply to gender-specific roles or just to marriage or parenting; we see it in the jobs of ministries we have, the opportunities God gives us, and in the life circumstances around us. Keep in mind, as seasons of life change and we mature, our callings/jobs/roles will change and develop with us. In addition, as we grow in our relationship with the Lord, He provides avenues for us to further explore and use our gifts in different ways.

In 1967, Martin Luther King Jr. famously delivered a speech at a junior high in Pennsylvania answering the question "What is your life's blueprint?" At one point, he says this:

> If it falls your lot to be a street sweeper, sweep streets like Michelangelo painted pictures, sweep streets like Beethoven composed music, sweep streets like Leontyne Price sings before the Metropolitan Opera. Sweep streets like Shakespeare wrote poetry. Sweep streets so well that all the hosts of heaven and earth will have to pause and say: Here lived a great street sweeper who swept his job well.[37]

Whatever role God has given you, whatever job He has set before you, and whatever He has called you to do, do it to the best of your ability for the glory of God.

KNOW WHEN TO SAY YES

When we are aware of our spiritual gifts and know what role God has called us to fulfill, it makes knowing what it is we are supposed to do with our days much clearer. Look for opportunities to say yes when you know it will allow you to use your gifts. Tackle projects and tasks within your job or role with joy knowing you're doing what it is God has called you to do. And at every point, be open to the Spirit's promptings to redirect or lead you as He wills.

Here are a few practical ways to put these principles into practice:

IDENTIFY YOUR SPIRITUAL GIFTS

Use one or more of the ways to know your spiritual gifts from above and start asking God what your gifts are. Ask for wisdom and discernment and open your ears and heart to hear from Him.

FIND ONE WAY TO USE YOUR GIFT

Start small, but be intentional in looking for service opportunities in your church or community where you can put your gifts to use. If you have the spiritual gift of hospitality, invite a new family to your home this week. If you have the spiritual gift of music, see if there's an opportunity for you to serve on the worship team. If you have the spiritual gift of shepherding, consider starting a discipleship group or meeting regularly with someone around you to intentionally discuss spiritual things.

BE A GREAT STREET SWEEPER

No matter how menial, redundant, or insignificant your role may feel, it has great potential to be a spiritual act of obedience and worship to God. Ask God to change your heart and equip you to be a great wife/surgeon/artist/businesswoman/teacher/homemaker/street sweeper for His glory.

Knowing that God has given us spiritual gifts and a role to fulfill changes everything. You don't have to do it all. Instead, do what God has laid before you today: nothing more, nothing less.

QUESTIONS FOR REFLECTION

1. *How would you define "spiritual gifts"? Do you believe your definition aligns with what we see in Scripture?*

2. *What is your spiritual gift? How are you using it to build up the body?*

3. *Are you fulfilling your role? What does this look like for you on a day-to-day basis?*

VERSE TO MEMORIZE

As each has received a gift, use it to serve one another, as good stewards of God's varied grace.

—1 PETER 4:10

CHAPTER TEN

SURRENDER CONTROL

But I trust in you, O LORD; I say, "You are my God."
My times are in your hand.

PSALM 31:14–15A

In the fall of 2014, Dustin and I headed to the airport with several other members of our church set to board a plane to South Asia.

For both of us, short-term mission trips had been a priority before we were married, and we knew we wanted to make them a priority after marriage as well. We were less than a year into marriage, and even though buying two plane tickets was a stretch financially and we were both short on available vacation days, we decided to go, trusting the Lord would both use us and teach us while we were there.

As I've previously mentioned, throughout my life I've struggled with a deep desire to control circumstances and people around me. So as I entered that airport, I had a plan, an itemized agenda, and an unspoken idea of what I expected God to do.

Well, as God often does, He crumbled my plans and expectations just minutes after we passed through security. As our team looked up at the flight board, we saw the word every traveler dreads: "delayed."

No big deal, I thought. *It will just be a little bit and we have a long layover before our international flight.* However, as I sat and watched the clock, the delay became longer and longer and we soon learned our plane wouldn't be coming until the next day.

Outwardly, I appeared maybe a little anxious but calm overall. But inwardly, I was a mess. I was trying to think of ways I could manipulate the situation. Maybe I could talk to different airlines. Maybe I could call the airport where our plane was stranded and get them to send a different one. Maybe I could call a friend whose dad is a pilot and see if he could pull some strings. Maybe we could drive to a nearby airport and catch a plane there. I realize now how extreme some of these thoughts were, but at the time I was desperate, grasping at straws. But the truth is, there was nothing I could do. It was out of my control.

CONTROL AND HURRY

Control and hurry are two sides of the same sword. Both reveal a lack of trust in the sovereignty and faithfulness of the Lord and instead take on a "me" mindset—a mindset that says my agenda, my plans, and my desires are more important than the bigger picture of God's eternal work.

How do you react when you feel like you've lost control over a situation in your life? Are you quick to surrender and submit to the Lord's will? Or, as I did, do you hold on for dear life and try to manipulate situations with little to no success?

As you continue reading through this chapter, here's what I ultimately want you to understand: Control is more of an illusion than a reality. We think it's something we can obtain or hold on to, but it will always be outside of our grasp. Okay, keep reading!

After receiving the news, my team ended up leaving the airport.

We all headed back to our respective homes to get another night of sleep, and made plans to return to the airport in the morning. Ultimately, we did make it to South Asia and only then saw little glimpses of why the Lord wanted our team to arrive a day late. The extra day allowed the team on the field to get some needed rest and still have extra time to put an evangelistic strategy into place. As a result, we saw a lot of spiritual fruit during our time there.

However, in my own heart, the Lord was continuing to do the work of helping me relinquish my tight grip on control. Over and over, I was pushed out of my comfort zone, placed in situations where I was completely at the mercy of others, and stripped of all plans and expectations. I was forced to slow down and take things as they came.

Margin, at its core, involves conceding control. As we create intentional time for the Lord to use us, we ultimately surrender the illusion of control we think we have over our days. This chapter is a call to sacrifice the control we cling to and replace it with a faith and a trust that acknowledges the Lord alone holds our future.

If you struggle with control, the good news is we have examples of people in the Bible who have learned to lay this desire down at the feet of Jesus.

ANXIOUS AND TROUBLED

If there's someone in the New Testament who epitomizes the picture of living hurried and desperately trying to remain in control, it would be Martha. If you're not familiar with the story of Martha and her sister in Luke 10:38–42, here's a quick paraphrase:

Jesus came to visit two sisters, Martha and Mary. Martha worked hard to prepare the house and serve Jesus, but Mary chose to sit and listen to Jesus' teaching. When Martha, clearly frustrated, approached Jesus about Mary not helping, Jesus commended Mary and reprimanded Martha for being "anxious and troubled about many things."

I can't count the number of times I've heard or studied this story over the years, often narrowing in on either Mary's devotion or Martha's anxiety. But as I studied this story through the lens of control, the Lord revealed so much more depth in the hearts of these women: depths I've seen mirrored back in my own heart.

First off, it's important for us to understand who these two sisters were before we start evaluating their actions. We see a little more of their stories and their character in John 11 and 12. We learn they live in Bethany and have a brother named Lazarus (yes, the same Lazarus Jesus raised from the dead). Many theologians believe Martha was the oldest sibling, then Mary, and then Lazarus. We also learn a little about them individually.

Martha's faith was put on display in John 11:20–27. After her brother had died, Martha met Jesus and acknowledged His power over death, His power to resurrect, and confessed Jesus is "the Christ, the Son of God, who is coming into the world." These are big words of devotion and faith in the middle of Jesus' ministry when many were still unsure of who He was. Martha also welcomed Jesus into her home back in the Luke passage and spent time serving Him—both of which were acts of love toward her Savior.

Mary also displayed great faith, just in different ways than Martha. When Martha went to meet Jesus after Lazarus' death, Mary stayed in the house mourning. But when she got up and went a little later, she fell at the feet of Jesus. In fact, we see her at Jesus' feet multiple times in these few passages. Mary even anointed His feet with expensive perfume and wiped them with her hair in John 12:3. During these days, the act of sitting at someone's feet was an act of submission. Like an apprentice who acknowledged the expertise of their teacher, sitting at one's feet displayed a desire to learn from them and to follow their lead.

Both Martha and Mary clearly loved Jesus and followed Him as disciples, which is part of what makes Martha's need for control so relatable. She wasn't seeking to live apart from Jesus, and she wasn't intentionally choosing a path of sin, she just had missed what was most important: Jesus above everything.

When Jesus arrived at her house, Martha understandably became distracted with trying to make everything perfect for Him. I don't know about you, but when I know someone is coming over or I have a friend stopping by, I definitely start trying to pick up and clean and prepare food or drinks in an attempt to make the person feel welcome and comfortable. This isn't what is wrong.

> **It comes down to this: If you claim Jesus as Lord but attempt to boss Him around, you aren't surrendering to His lordship over your life.**

However, what is wrong is when distraction and control turn our hearts bitter and angry, or we are trying to impress our guests, rather than serve them.

Martha became critical of Mary and even frustrated with Jesus for His inaction. Look at her words to Jesus: "And she went up to him and said, 'Lord, do you not care that my sister has left me to serve alone? Tell her then to help me" (Luke 10:40b).

Can you hear the annoyance and accusation in her voice? I wasn't there, and we don't have documentation of every minute leading up to this conversation, but I have a feeling this anger had been building and burning in her heart. Each minute that Mary sat while Martha cleaned, served, and prepared gave her more fuel for the fire.

Examine Jesus' response though:

> But the Lord answered her, "Martha, Martha, you are
> anxious and troubled about many things, but one thing is
> necessary. Mary has chosen the good portion, which will not
> be taken away from her." (Luke 10:41–42)

Oof. Do those words hit you like they hit me?

"Only one thing is necessary." What was the one thing? Time at the feet of Jesus.

It comes down to this: If you claim Jesus as Lord but attempt to boss Him around, you aren't surrendering to His lordship over your life.

When, like Martha, our attempt to control even good things (like welcoming Jesus into your house) becomes a priority over abiding with our Savior, it's time to slow down and reprioritize.

This is what we learn from David in Psalm 31.

MY TIMES ARE IN YOUR HAND

David knew what it was to wait on the Lord, to surrender his control, and to trust that the Lord's purposes were greater. From tending sheep as a shepherd to ruling over Israel as king, David experienced God's faithfulness and sovereignty. And in the midst of trouble, here was his cry: "But I trust in you, O LORD; I say, 'You are my God.' My times are in your hand" (Ps. 31:14–15a)

When I feel the urge to control the situations around me, I cling to this verse. Our times are in His hand. We can't add a single minute to our life, or control the number of our days, but we can surrender to the One who can. This surrender brings peace and freedom. If we trust God is who He says He is, there is no better place to be than in the hand of God.

Later in David's life when he took an unauthorized census, God let him choose his punishment from three options: three years of famine, fleeing from his enemies for three months, or three days of pestilence, the one he ultimately chose (2 Sam. 24). I love that he chose the one that set him firmly in God's hand.

> "I am in great distress. Let us fall into the hand of the LORD, for his mercy is great; but let me not fall into the hand of man." (2 Sam. 24:14)

What about you? Are you striving to trust God wholeheartedly despite the ongoing struggle of the flesh to control? Are you making choices to daily surrender your desire for control to Him? Have you considered the peace and freedom that is yours when you choose to stand firm in the sovereign hands of the Lord? He is merciful and holds your time in His hand.

How do we do this in the day-to-day though? What does it look like to make decisions that reflect our faith in God's sovereignty?

We ask God to enable us, through the power of the Holy Spirit, to surrender our desire for control to Him as a habit or way of life.

CONTROL AND DECISION-MAKING

At times, decision-making has paralyzed me. What if I make the wrong choice? What if this isn't what God has for me? I even see this manifest in small choices throughout my day. Should I prepare the beef or the chicken for dinner? Do I order the white command hooks or the silver command hooks? (Yes, I really did agonize over this!)

Often this "analysis paralysis" is rooted in a deeper fear of losing control. It's a heart issue that reveals deep-seated pride. It exposes my wrong belief that I can somehow "mess up" God's plan. Not only is this belief a lie, but it actually hinders my witness, weakens my faith, and seeks to place limits on a limitless God.

Recently I studied the story of Samson, and I saw so much of myself in his mother. Samson wanted to marry a Philistine woman, which was in direct disobedience of the Law. As we tend to do when our kids are making a poor decision, his parents objected and offered alternative solutions (in this case, marry any Israelite woman).

Decision-making should not lead to fear.

But then Scripture says this: "His father and mother didn't realize the LORD was at work in this, creating an opportunity to work against the Philistines, who ruled over Israel at that time" (Judg. 14:4).

God had bigger plans for Samson's choice. His poor decision wasn't going to affect God's purposes. In fact, God was going to use it to accomplish them!

Often in Scripture, we see God bringing about His will despite the sin nature in the heart of men. Even still, there is no wisdom in presuming upon God's grace and sovereignty by making willfully poor choices. Even Paul asks in Romans 6:1b–2, "Are we to continue in sin that grace may abound? By no means! How can we who died to sin still live in it?"

Yes, our decisions have consequences, and yes, we should always seek wisdom from God in making them, but decision-making should not lead to fear. God desires to use us knowing full well His purposes will ultimately be accomplished! He is sovereign, in control of all things all the time.

I know this can be hard to understand and that's okay, but it doesn't diminish the truth of God's Word. We can feel vulnerable and be tempted to doubt God's Word when we don't fully understand it. This is the time to be even more mindful of the ways we grasp for the illusion of control. Instead, this actually presents an opportunity for us to trust Him more.

So, if decision-making shouldn't bring fear but still has to be done, how can we make the best decision while still surrendering control? Here are a few practical steps:

INTIMATELY KNOW WHAT GOD COMMANDS

If a choice that would directly go against God's Word is an option, the decision should be easy to make—our answer is no, even if that choice may seem momentarily appealing. However, this means we not only need to know what the Bible says, but we also need to be attentive to the Spirit's promptings.

LOVE PEOPLE

When faced with a decision that seems to be in a gray zone or hard to make, pause and determine how it will affect those around you. Will it cause harm to anyone, even if it's just to their feelings? Will it cause a brother or sister weaker or younger in the faith to stumble? Could it harm your witness? If so, take heed!

SEEK WISDOM

God promises us wisdom if we will seek it. Run to His Word. Ask other believers who have walked similar paths before you. Pray for discernment. Wisdom always provides clarity.

TAKE A STEP

If the decision in front of you doesn't go against God's commands, doesn't harm those around you, and has been wisely evaluated, then take a step and ask God to clearly open and close doors.

For example, shortly after I had my firstborn, I agonized over if I should change jobs or not. I loved what I did but also had little flexibility and worked set hours at a desk all day. With a little encouragement from my husband, I started to step forward, asking God for clarity. I met with my boss and asked if I could work from home part-time. His answer was eventually no, and that door closed. So I took a different step. I applied to a company that allowed employees to work remotely. Door after door opened, and it wasn't long before I was working fully at home. Circumstances are not always this black and white, but God is always faithful to direct our steps if we will walk in faith.

We can confidently make the decisions in front of us if we recognize and submit to God at every point.

What about you? How do you make decisions, big or little, when you feel stuck?

If you have a decision in front of you today, seek wisdom, take a step, and ask God to use you as He works. He is in control!

RELINQUISH CONTROL

Giving up control is hard. But knowing who is in control makes it a little easier. There is great freedom and goodness that comes with living in submission to the Lord's will.

In *The Cost of Control*, Sharon Hodde Miller expresses it this way: "The only time in human history when perfect freedom and peace existed in the world was not the absence of boundaries, but within them."[38]

Just like choosing to eat from the tree in the garden of Eden, control may seem appealing. But also like the choice to take the fruit from that tree, it leads to destruction. It will always demand more power, more knowledge, and more self-centered thinking.

Here's the beauty though: when we hand over the little control we think we have to an Almighty God, we gain the freedom and the peace He intends for us. The confines are there for our good. Control opposes limits but submission recognizes the freedom of boundaries.

As promised, this book is designed to provide practical applications and processes we can implement. Here are a few ways to concede control as you go about your day.

Prioritize the "One Necessary Thing"

Just like Mary, choose to sit at the feet of Jesus. Spend time dwelling on His sovereignty, laying down your fears and anxieties, and confessing your desire to control what you shouldn't. This may involve time in the Word, prayer, silence, or even listening to worship music. Don't let the temporary get in the way of the significant.

Know Who Holds You in His Hand

It's not belittling or self-deprecating to recognize how small you are and how big God is. You have great value to God, but you are not big enough or powerful enough to even put a dent in His plans or purposes. Recognize who He is and who you are when you try to control circumstances around you.

Practice Wise Decision-Making

If like me you struggle with "analysis paralysis," start practicing wise decision-making with the small things, so you'll be prepared when big decisions stand before you. Know His commands, love people, seek wisdom, and then take a step.

Will you surrender control today?

THE END IN SIGHT

As we close out the second part of the book, my prayer is that the processes and tools we've identified have equipped you to further live surrendered to God's will and plan for your life. I hope your desire and love for Him has grown and that you are already establishing rhythms and routines designed to make room in your schedule for the Lord to work. However, this isn't the end.

The third and final part of this book breaks down practices and applications designed to help us become more and more Christlike day by day. If you're still asking, "Where do I start?" "Is there actually a time to hurry?" "What should my schedule look like?" "What happens when I fail?"—keep going. Keep reading, keep praying, and keep seeking the Lord. An unhurried life is worth it.

QUESTIONS FOR REFLECTION

1. *How do you react when situations feel out of control? How should you react?*

2. *Would you consider yourself to be more like Mary or Martha? What do you need to eliminate from your life so that you can prioritize what's most important?*

3. *What decisions do you have in front of you right now? How can you practice wise decision-making and surrender to God's control?*

VERSE TO MEMORIZE

But I trust in you, O LORD; I say, "You are my God."
My times are in your hand.

—PSALM 31:14–15A

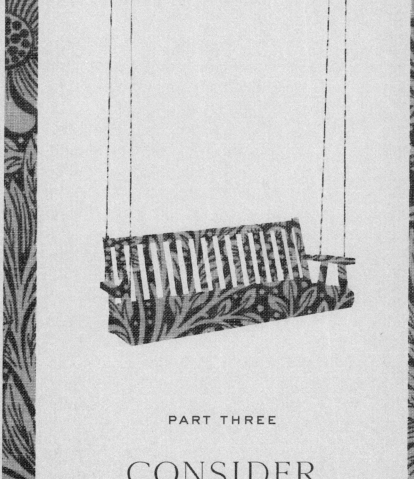

PART THREE

CONSIDER
YOUR WAYS

CHAPTER ELEVEN

LITTLE BY LITTLE

For everyone who lives on milk is unskilled in the word of righteousness, since he is a child. But solid food is for the mature, for those who have their powers of discernment trained by constant practice to distinguish good from evil.

HEBREWS 5:13–14

Reluctantly and still half-asleep, I rolled over as I heard the all-too-familiar "pat, pat, pat, pat, swooooossshhh" sound coming into our bedroom. Even at four years old, my son still managed to wake in the night and quietly walk into our room dragging his beloved stuffed lamb named "Lovey" behind him.

After months of re-sleep-training, doctor's calls, sleepless nights on the floor in his room, and gallons of coffee, my husband and I caved and started pulling him into our bed . . . definitely not a fate we happily accepted. But my perspective changed after a conversation with a dear older friend.

With wisdom and love in her eyes, she said, "One day will be the last day he sleeps in your bed. You used to change his diapers, and now he's potty-trained. You used to nurse him, and now he eats what you eat. You used to carry him, and now he runs literally everywhere he goes. He's growing, and will grow out of this too."

She was right. As a mom, I've seen the coming and going of seasons in my children's lives, and I've seen the growth she referenced. But as I continued to come back to her words, the Lord gently reminded me it's not only my children who need growth. As a follower of Jesus, I also need to grow as I walk through different spiritual seasons.[39]

This growth, including the growth necessary to live unhurried, surrendering our plans for His purposes, is a process. One we must take step by step.

As I continued to reflect on my friend's insights, these words from Hebrews 5:13–14 flooded my mind:

> For everyone who lives on milk is unskilled in the word of righteousness, since he is a child. But solid food is for the mature, for those who have their powers of discernment trained by constant practice to distinguish good from evil.

When it comes to living unhurried, it's important to realize that growth happens over time.

Here, the author of Hebrews almost scolds his Jewish-Christian audience for their lack of maturity. He writes they should be teachers by this point, but instead need to be taught (5:12). They are still drinking milk when instead they should eat solid food. Their lives are marked by stagnation and spiritual immaturity.

What about you? The Bible is a believer's guidebook for developing spiritual maturity. As you are spending time in the Word, are you developing skills in better recognizing the differences between what God says is right and wrong? Are you drinking milk when you should be eating meat? Have you grown to the point where you're seeking to consistently place the Lord's priorities over your plans?

The beauty of growth is that it doesn't happen immediately. Growth is a hard-fought process defined by Christ-centered determination and dependence on the One who is our foundation and source of strength. It is a moment-by-moment decision to pursue things of the Lord instead of things of the world. Growth is slow, steady, and only truly visible on the other side of the season.

You may be happy to know my son eventually learned to sleep in his room again (the secret was bunk beds with his brother and a fish tank as a night light, if you're a desperate parent). However, it happened little by little.

When it comes to living unhurried, it's important to realize this type of growth also happens over time. Unless we pack our bags and move to a monastery overnight (which I don't recommend), our lives won't naturally slow down. We must make choices and changes day by day, moment by moment.

The good news is, according to God's Word, one step of obedience after another is glorifying and honoring to Him.

DIP YOUR TOE

Often, in the Old Testament, the Lord gave instructions to His people one step at a time. It was only when they had completed the step that they knew what to do next.

Shortly after the death of Moses, Joshua assumed command of the Israelites who had been wandering in the desert, and the Lord gave him instructions to cross the Jordan River and enter the promised land.

Joshua knew enemies awaited him beyond the river, but he also knew this land was promised to his people. But the first step to conquering and living in the place God had designed for them was to cross the river.

I obviously wasn't there, but I can imagine it was somewhat of a chaotic scene. Mothers looking around taking headcounts of all their children, calling out names. Kids yelling, running, and constantly asking, "How much longer?" Men carrying large loads including their tents and family's belongings. The overwhelming noise of people, animals, and now, rushing water. Crossing the river must have felt daunting.

> So when the people set out from their tents to pass over the Jordan with the priests bearing the ark of the covenant before the people, and as soon as those bearing the ark had come as far as the Jordan, **and the feet of the priests bearing the ark were dipped in the brink of the water** (now the Jordan overflows all its banks throughout the time of harvest), the waters coming down from above stood and rose up in a heap very far away. . . . And the people passed over opposite Jericho. (Josh. 3:14–16)

Did you catch that? It was only when the feet of the priests were dipped in the water that the water stopped flowing.

Scripture doesn't tell us if those priests were reluctant or fearful or hesitant, but it does tell us their feet had to enter the water first. I think if it was me, I would've felt much more confident if the raging water stopped and cleared for me before I had to step in. However, it's the first dipping of a toe that displays true obedience. They were willing to step in, trusting the Lord would make a way even as the water flowed.

Are you standing in front of a raging river when it comes to the chaos and pace of your life? Does it feel like there's no way the water will part to allow you to pass through? Maybe it's time to dip your toe.

Dipping your toe into an unhurried life could look like:

Setting a timer to spend several minutes in prayer each morning before reaching for your phone.

Saying no to just one thing this week.

Initiating a conversation with a friend at a time that feels inconvenient for you.

Scheduling one hour of "free" time. Or, in other words, designating a time to be open to whatever God has for you.

Choosing the longest line at the grocery store and praying for the people in front of you.

These aren't massive life changes or drastic measures to take, but they are small steps of obedience that reflect growth and a desire to pursue God's purposes above your own.

ONE STEP AT A TIME

Shortly after the Israelites crossed the Jordan, they found themselves facing yet another huge obstacle: Jericho.

From the time I was little, I've always loved the story of the fall of Jericho. I vividly remember marching around my Sunday school room singing, "Joshua fought the battle of Jericho, Jericho, Jericho . . ."[40] and then quickly falling on the ground as I sang, "And the walls came tumbling down!"

Not only that, but to this day, thanks to the VeggieTales episode "Josh and the Big Wall,"[41] I still picture sarcastic French peas dropping purple slushies on the vegetable army while singing, "It's plain to see your brains are very small to think walking will be knocking down our wall." (Anyone else grow up on VeggieTales?!)

But, I have an inkling the way the cute Sunday school songs and entertaining VeggieTales episode portray this event is a far cry from what actually happened. In reality, Jericho was a fortress.

Here's how pastor Alan Carr described the city: "Jericho is known as the oldest city in the world. In Joshua's day, it was surrounded by a system of two massive stone walls. The outer wall was 6 feet thick and about 20 feet high. The inner wall was about 12 feet thick and was 30 feet high. Between the walls was a guarded walkway about 15 feet wide. Israel's problem was that they had a city to conquer, but there were some extremely huge walls in the way."[42]

> I want things to happen immediately. Some days, I don't want to get up and march, and yet I want the walls to fall.

Take a minute to picture yourself in the Israelites' shoes—or sandals, as the case may be. They had seen God do miraculous things, like stop the water of the Jordan, and knew God had provided this land, but the obstacle in front of them was huge. I imagine at least some of them were fearful, uncertain, and even confused about if this was really what God had planned.

But God told Joshua, "See, I have given Jericho into your hand" (Josh. 6:2). Now, the people just had to decide if they were going to obey. Chances are you're familiar with what God told them to do. The people were to march around the city for six days, and then march around the city seven times on the seventh day. Then, they were to shout loudly and if they did this, God promised "the wall of the city will fall down flat" (Josh. 6:5).

This was all the information they had. God asked them to obey, not dependent on their feelings in the moment or their personal desires, but on their devotion to Him.

The walls of Jericho only fell because the people chose obedience step after step. Each day they had to wake up and choose to walk. God had told them what He would do, but their obedience was required.

Here's where I struggle, and maybe you do too: I want things to happen immediately. Some days, I don't want to get up and march, and yet I want the walls to fall.

So often, God's timing is not our timing. We've looked at how He's sovereign, and we've seen how His ways are best, but if we are truly going to live like we know this to be true, we have to take the steps. One day after another, we have to march, trusting God will do what He says He will do.

This is the process of becoming like Jesus.

SANCTIFICATION IS A PROCESS

If you've been around the "church world" for any length of time, there's a good chance you've heard the word "sanctification." Sanctification simply means the ongoing transformation of our hearts and lives to become like Jesus. It's the process of being made holy. But it's just that: a process.

Remember how I mentioned I've always been somewhat of a perfectionist? Well, part of being a perfectionist involves wanting to be perfect right away.

When I attempted to learn to play piano as a child, I wanted to go from not knowing where to put my hands on the keys to becoming a star pianist. I would listen to my nana play everything from Beethoven's *Moonlight Sonata* to Scott Joplin's ragtime music and want to be like her. But she had spent years playing, and I was just starting. To make it worse, I hated practicing. When I practiced, I would (obviously) make mistakes, and this served to further remind me just how much I wasn't perfect. Then, because I didn't like practicing, I didn't improve. Like most things in life, learning to play piano is a process requiring discipline, commitment, and perseverance.

Sanctification, or the process of becoming like Jesus, requires these things, too. But before we dig in much deeper, I want to offer a little clarity to make sure we are all on the same page. Here's a quick breakdown:

Salvation (sometimes called positional sanctification or justification) happens the moment you admit to Jesus you're a sinner, believe Jesus is the Son of God, and confess your faith in Him as Lord of your life (John 3:16). Or, as our children's pastor teaches the kids: you ask Jesus to be the boss of your life. For the one who genuinely makes this profession and experiences true heart change, at that very moment, your eternity with the Lord is secured forever (John 10:28–29).

Sanctification (or progressive sanctification) is the process of becoming holy or like Jesus, as we are focusing on in this chapter. From our salvation until the time Jesus calls us home, this is where we are (Phil. 1:6).

Glorification (or perfect sanctification) is a one-time event that will happen when we stand before God, holy because of the blood of Jesus (Phil. 3:20–21).

It's progressive sanctification that requires us to move forward gradually, recognizing that little steps, with our eyes on Jesus, are actually big decisions in becoming more and more like Christ.

Take a look at what Paul said:

> Not that I have already obtained this or am already perfect, but I press on to make it my own, because Christ Jesus has made me his own. Brothers, I do not consider that I have made it my own. But one thing I do: forgetting what lies behind and straining forward to what lies ahead, I press on toward the goal for the prize of the upward call of God in Christ Jesus. (Phil. 3:12–14)

This is the same Paul whose mission was sharing the gospel. He knew he couldn't and wouldn't ever fully obtain the righteousness of Christ while he was on this earth, because he's not Christ. And neither are we! But does this mean we just give up like I did with the piano? Absolutely not. I may never play the piano, but I pray I am never found giving up on the pursuit of Christlikeness. There is joy in following Jesus!

Paul "strained forward to what lies ahead" and "pressed on toward the goal" because the "prize of the upward call of God in Christ Jesus" is worth it.

Here's the thing: The little decisions to pursue Christlikeness are birthed out of a deep love for Him. Once we realize the magnitude of what Jesus has done for us, we will want to live our lives as a reflection of that same love.

But what if we decide not to pursue holiness? Here's what theologian and author D. A. Carson says in *For the Love of God*:

> People do not drift toward holiness. Apart from grace-driven effort, people do not gravitate toward godliness, prayer, and obedience to Scripture, faith, and delight in the Lord. We drift toward compromise and call it tolerance; we drift toward disobedience and call it freedom; we drift toward superstition and call it faith. We cherish the indiscipline of lost self-control and call it relaxation; we slouch toward prayerlessness and delude ourselves into thinking we have escaped legalism; we slide toward godlessness and convince ourselves we have been liberated.[43]

Are you drifting? This is one of the reasons why it's so crucial we slow down and remove the distractions we are so prone to dwell on. When my life is about me, it sure makes it a lot harder to live my life looking like Him.

MOVING TOWARD MATURITY

What does it look like to be "spiritually mature"?

As I pondered this question, I started thinking about people in my life who I consider to be amazing men and women of faith. One of the biggest characteristics I could identify in each of them is that their outward self mirrors their inner self. By that, I mean their actions consistently align with and reflect their heart. They each bear the fruit of the Spirit we see in Galatians 5:22–23. "But the fruit of the Spirit is love, joy, peace, patience, kindness, goodness, faithfulness, gentleness, self-control; against such things there is no law."

I love this passage and at one point took a deep dive into what bearing each fruit looks like practically in our lives. Because of time, I won't unpack this here, but I've included a resource in the back of this book to help you examine your fruit-bearing. Please use it to reference as the Lord leads. For example, if you know God is asking you to wait patiently, take a look at the indicators of patience, and ask Him to help you take steps toward maturity in that area. Or if you know gentleness is an area you struggle with, reference the indicators and pursue just one thing in that area today.

Spiritual maturity comes when we keep our eyes on eternity and choose small steps of obedience day by day. These daily acts of obedience are not insignificant or meaningless; they are small, necessary steps in a larger walk marked by faith and Christlikeness.

Ready to put it into practice? Here are a few practical steps to get you started.

PICK UP A FORK

Remember how Paul accused the new believers of continuing to drink milk when they should be eating meat? If you're stuck in a similar pattern, it's time to put down the milk, pick up a fork, and start eating meat, bite by bite. This means you stop depending on others to spiritually feed you. Listening to your pastor preach or your Sunday school teacher teach you on Sunday mornings is not enough. What are you doing to learn more about who Jesus is and how He wants you to live? Spend time in the Word, draw near to Him in prayer, and abide with Him throughout your day. This will begin to nourish your soul and give you strength for the mission at hand.

DIP YOUR TOE

Another way to pursue spiritual maturity is to start by dipping your toe, just like the priests did. Focus on one spiritual discipline (remember chapter 7), and then another. Don't try to do it all. Instead, ask God what one thing He wants you to do to become more like Him today or this week. This, too, is part of the process.

START MARCHING

If you want to continue in the process of becoming holy, you've got to start and keep marching into the calling He has on your life. God asked the Israelites to take step after step as an act of obedience. We too, need to take steps of obedience. Our daily marching can look different depending on our circumstances or season of life. God understands the struggles, weaknesses, and temptations that challenge our ability and desire to march, and He meets us there with grace in our time of need (Hebrews 4:15–16). The sweetest part is He's with us when we are tired or hurt or discouraged, offering His strength if we will rely fully on Him. So take one step and then another and then another. You are not alone!

Will you slow down, surrender your plans, and take small steps of obedience today?

QUESTIONS FOR REFLECTION

1. *Can you identify evidence of spiritual growth in your life? What areas do you need to focus on next?*

2. *Do you struggle with wanting things to happen immediately? How can you wait well today?*

3. *Would you consider yourself spiritually mature? Why or why not?*

VERSE TO MEMORIZE

I press on toward the goal for the prize
of the upward call of God in Christ Jesus.

—PHILIPPIANS 3:14

CHAPTER TWELVE

KNOW WHEN
TO HURRY

Behold, now is the favorable time;
behold, now is the day of salvation.

2 CORINTHIANS 6:2B

I vividly remember the sense of calm I had about me.

On January 12, 2019, I felt a familiar twinge in my abdomen. At thirty-seven weeks pregnant with my second child, I knew exactly what it was: a contraction. I looked around and saw my almost two-year-old playing with his favorite trucks and my husband leisurely enjoying his Saturday morning. I wasn't panicked, I wasn't afraid, I was just acutely aware this day would change my life forever.

Unlike my first labor experience, this time I knew when to hurry. The first time, everything felt urgent. I called my doctor's office during my first contraction, raced home from work, wanted to go to the hospital immediately, and quickly learned that labor doesn't work that way. However, this time, I wanted to take it slow. I wanted to enjoy these last minutes at home as a family of three. I wanted to remember the details and appreciate the experience. And I wanted to prep my house for homecoming with a baby (I know—very type A of me).

As soon as I confirmed I was in active labor, I began to clean. My kind husband wanted nothing more than to get in the car and rush to the hospital, but I knew I would feel better coming home to a picked-up house. As Dustin paced and tried his best to hurry me along, I worked intentionally and methodically, listening to my body along the way. When the task was done and I knew it was time, we drove to the hospital to meet our second son.

The truth is, there is a time to hurry. Ambulances fly down the highway in emergencies, people run through airports in attempts to catch their planes, and parents rush to the aid of a child in need. Not only that, but when it comes to eternity, we share the gospel with urgency, not knowing how long we each have on earth.

Slowing down, creating margin, and resting in the Lord is biblical, foundational, and what this book is about. But what if we need to know how to hurry too? How can we learn to slow down if we don't also know how and when to hurry well?

A BIBLICAL EXAMPLE OF HURRY

In 1 Samuel 25, we read the story of a discerning woman named Abigail and her harsh, badly behaved husband, Nabal.

After the death of Samuel, David and his men were in the wilderness of Paran and in need of food and water. Previously, they had been alongside Nabal's shepherds and had treated them well, so when David sent his men to ask Nabal for provisions, he also expected to be treated graciously. However, that's not what happened.

Instead, Nabal insulted David and his lineage, disregarded the kindness shown to his shepherds, and selfishly refused to provide for David's men. As a result, David and his men prepared to go to battle against Nabal.

When Abigail heard what was happening, she acted wisely, courageously, and hurriedly. "Then Abigail **made haste** and took two hundred loaves and two skins of wine and five sheep already prepared and five seahs of parched grain and a hundred clusters of raisins and two hundred cakes of figs, and laid them on donkeys. And she said to her young men, 'Go on before me; behold, I come after you.' But she did not tell her husband Nabal" (1 Sam. 25:18–19).

As soon as Abigail reached David, she "**hurried** and got down from the donkey" (v. 23), bowed before him, took ownership, and begged for forgiveness. David responded in this way:

> "Blessed be the LORD, the God of Israel, who sent you this day to meet me! Blessed be your discretion, and blessed be you, who have kept me this day from bloodguilt and from working salvation with my own hand! For as surely as the LORD, the God of Israel, lives, who has restrained me from hurting you, **unless you had hurried** and come to meet me, truly by morning there had not been left to Nabal so much as one male." (1 Sam. 25:32b–34)

The story ends with God striking Nabal down and Abigail humbly and willingly becoming David's wife.

Abigail's hurry righted a wrong, helped to prevent further sin and wrongdoing, and changed her life's trajectory. She rightly acted with urgency.

However, if there's anything to be learned from Abigail's hurry, it's that wisdom and discretion accompanied it.

Even before we learn of Abigail's act, Scripture describes her as "discerning" (v. 3). Discerning is defined as "showing insight and understanding." [44] She didn't allow being married to a wicked, foolish man influence her ability to practice wisdom, understanding, and righteousness. We don't know her full story, but we do know the Lord helped her decide right from wrong, truth from lies in this situation.

So, when she learned of Nabal's sin, she was able to wisely discern the right course of action, and then do it quickly.

What about you? Do you often react without gathering all the facts? Do you make rash decisions without first seeking wisdom or guidance? Do you hurry so often that everything always feels urgent?

If so, it may be time to stop and ask the Lord for discernment.

First Thessalonians 5:21 commands us to "test everything; hold fast what is good." Testing often requires time, facts, and wisdom; however, the resulting action can be done quickly and with urgency if it is of the Lord.

Abigail shows us the value of pairing hurry with discernment and the need to hurry in order to correct a wrong, but are there other reasons to hurry? What else does the Word of God say about acting with urgency?

KNOW WHEN TO HURRY

The Bible gives us three clear categories of times to practice hurry. Hopefully, as we understand these and apply them to our lives, we will be marked by righteous urgency instead of busyness.

Sharing the Gospel

In Scripture, the first and most prevalent reason we see to hurry is spiritual urgency. Without question, sharing the gospel should take priority over our schedules, time, and agendas because people's spiritual destinations are always at stake.

But what does it actually mean to "share the gospel"? First and foremost, it encompasses sharing the basics of salvation and the good news of Jesus Christ. Even more than that though, sharing the gospel is an intentional lifestyle where we are making the most of every opportunity the Lord puts before us. Sometimes we plant seeds by teaching others about who Jesus is. Other times we water as we walk through life with someone pointing them to a relationship with Jesus. I know this can create pressure, but remember, ultimately God is the one who calls a sinner to salvation (1 Cor. 3:6–7). It's a privilege that He chooses to use us, so stay alert and willing.

I'm so thankful I had people in my life who believed this wholeheartedly and lived it out around me. From the time I was born, my parents, grandparents, and friends made it a point to share the gospel with me regularly. I truly believe it's because of their faithfulness, consistency, and urgency that Christ called me to follow Him at a young age.

One night as I was getting ready for bed, I found a little booklet that explains the good news of Jesus, lying around my house. This wasn't necessarily unusual because my dad regularly went out visiting as part of the evangelism team at our church. This team would visit church guests or people who had expressed interest in learning about Jesus and share the gospel with them. But this time, out of my six-year-old curiosity, I picked the booklet up to practice my newfound reading skills and discovered much more. As I read, I felt God pulling at my heart like He had never done before. I immediately went and found my parents and told them that I knew that I needed to surrender my life to the Lord. They led me in a prayer of salvation, and in that prayer, I admitted my sinful nature and asked for forgiveness. I repented and told God that I wholeheartedly believed Jesus is God's Son and He lived a perfect life, died for me, and conquered death by rising again. That night in my childhood bedroom, I committed to give God control of my life to use for His glory.

God used a tract to capture my heart in those sweet and sacred moments, but the foundation was laid long before that. Sharing the gospel always matters.

Have you had an experience like this? Or did you come to faith in Christ when you were older? If you're not sure, I'd encourage you to reach out to a pastor or minister at a Bible-believing church to talk through it. God is always faithful to save.

BASICS OF THE GOSPEL

The gospel is simply the good news of Jesus Christ. From the time I was a child, I was taught the "ABCs of salvation." Maybe these can help you in believing and sharing too.

A: Admit that you're a sinner, in need of a Savior. Sin is anything we do say, think, or don't do that misses the mark of what God has asked of us (Rom. 3:23).

B: Believe that Jesus is God's Son who lived a perfect life, died on the cross for you, and rose again to give you new life (Rom. 5:8).

C: Confess your faith in Jesus as Savior and Lord and commit to live your life for Him (Rom. 10:9–10).

It's also important to know that when it comes to sharing the gospel, our job is obedience in sharing, no matter the outcome.

A friend and I recently had a conversation with a man whose son played basketball through our church's sports league. As we sat on his porch watching the beautiful Oklahoma sunset turn from yellow and orange to deep red and purple, we talked about our children and the church, but more importantly we talked about the good news of Jesus. He genuinely seemed interested and asked numerous questions about Jesus' life and our own responses to the gospel, but over and over his response was something like, "I'll just have to keep thinking about that." There was a lack of immediacy in his spirit, despite our urges that we aren't guaranteed tomorrow.

As night fell and we walked back to the car, I remember feeling both a peace and a deep sadness. I knew I had been obedient to share and that the Spirit had guided our conversation, but the man's lack of response was disheartening. My friend was so good to remind me that our job is to share urgently, and God will take care of the rest. We never know when planted seeds will bloom.

In John 9:4, Jesus explained spiritual urgency to His disciples like this: "We must work the works of him who sent me while it is day; night is coming, when no one can work."

Here's what it boils down to:

We must work while it's day. This means right now, while we are alive and able to share with those around us. We have a job to do and limited time to do it. How will you use the time you have?

Night is coming. Whether through death or Jesus' return, a time is coming when it will be too late. It's inevitable. And once night is here, we won't have more daylight to accomplish the tasks we wish we would've done. Faithfully act while there's still time.

Christian theologian Carl F. H. Henry put it like this, "The gospel is only good news if it gets there in time."[45]

> **You have the good news! Share it regularly. Share it faithfully. Share it now.**

Sharing the gospel will often involve putting God's purposes over your plans. He desires everyone to know Him and choose to follow Him (1 Tim. 2:3–4), and He desires to use you. It might not always be comfortable and definitely won't always be convenient, but it will always be worth it.

I love this reminder from Paul in Romans 10:14–15:

> How then will they call on him in whom they have not believed? And how are they to believe in him of whom they have never heard? And how are they to hear without someone preaching? And how are they to preach unless they are sent? As it is written, "How beautiful are the feet of those who preach the good news!"

You have the good news! Share it regularly. Share it faithfully. Share it now. "Behold, **now** is the favorable time; behold, **now** is the day of salvation" (2 Cor. 6:2b).

Obeying Quickly

Another reason for urgency we see outlined in Scripture is obedience. God speaks strongly about the importance of obeying Him in His Word. Here are a few examples:

> "If you love me, you will keep my commandments" (John 14:15).

> "Why do you call me 'Lord, Lord,' and not do what I tell you?" (Luke 6:46).

> "For this is the love of God, that we keep his commandments. And his commandments are not burdensome" (1 John 5:3).

Our obedience is founded on our love for Him. When we have an abiding, intimate relationship with Him, we will want to do as He asks, not just when it's convenient, but immediately.

Scripture is full of examples of people who are quick to obey. We regularly see phrases like: "On that very day . . ." "Immediately . . ." or "At once . . ."

But is that what we do? Do we have a sense of urgency when it comes to obeying God?

I think one of the clearest ways God has shown me the importance of immediate obedience has been through parenting. I can think of more times than I would like when I've frantically yelled at one of my kids to "stop!" as I've watched their ball roll out into the middle of the road the same time a car has come driving by. At that moment, their obedience is the single difference between a horrible, tragic ER trip and simply continuing on with a fun game of football/soccer/basketball/four-square.

This obviously is an extreme example, but the principle remains: God desires our immediate obedience. Why? Because He deeply loves us. He knows what's best for us. And He is at work in ways we may never fully see or understand. Our obedience is a reflection of our faith in Him.

Take a look at this example about the disciples in Matthew 4:18–22:

> While walking by the Sea of Galilee, he saw two brothers, Simon (who is called Peter) and Andrew his brother, casting a net into the sea, for they were fishermen. And he said to them, "Follow me, and I will make you fishers of men." **Immediately** they left their nets and followed him. And going on from there he saw two other brothers, James the son of Zebedee and John his brother, in the boat with Zebedee their father, mending their nets, and he called them. **Immediately** they left the boat and their father and followed him.

This is probably a story you've read before, but pause for a minute and really put yourself in their shoes. Fishing was their livelihood. It's likely what they had done for the majority of their lives. It was comfortable, familiar, and their means of provision. And yet, Scripture doesn't record any hesitation. They didn't ask how long they might be gone or what they should do with their boats. They didn't question if they were financially able to take a little work break or if they had the skills to do what Jesus might need them to do. Instead, they obeyed immediately. And this obedience changed both their present and their future.

Has there been a time in your life when God has clearly prompted you to do something? Maybe it was something monumental like quitting your job or moving to a new city, or maybe it was something lesser like talking to a stranger or canceling a specific plan. Did you obey right away, or did you question it? Looking back now, can you see why He may have asked you to obey?

I distinctly remember one December morning hearing the Lord's instructions as I stood in line at the store. I had been busy shopping for Christmas gifts and felt caught up in the hustle and bustle of the season. But, as I was making small talk with the cashier, I sensed the Lord asking me to give something to her. To be honest, I didn't want to. Our budget was stretched thin and I felt awkward, so I walked away, but the Lord persisted. Before I could even get out the door, I reluctantly turned around and went and purchased a gift card to that same store. As I walked up to the cashier again, I asked the Lord for peace and direction. I simply told her God had given me so much and I sensed Him calling me to give to her. Tears welled up in her eyes as she explained she didn't know how she would be able to buy her children anything for Christmas that year and had been praying that the Lord would provide. I'm so thankful He chose to use me.

Obedience isn't always easy. In fact, sometimes I feel like joining my toddler in his temper tantrum when I'm asked to do something

I don't want to do. However, obedience is always better, whether we can see God's "why" behind asking now or not.

A quick reminder: Even in this, there's grace. Yes, God wants us to obey immediately, but when we choose disobedience, this doesn't necessarily mean it's too late. He is a God of forgiveness. Sometimes the opportunity may have passed, but this gives us an opportunity to learn, repent, and ask God for future opportunities. And sometimes, the opportunity is still there. Don't delay obedience any longer. We should repent of our feet dragging and quickly move forward in obedience.

We don't need to live hurried lives (in case you haven't picked up on that yet), but when God speaks, we would be wise to obey with urgency. Don't wait, He knows what He's doing!

Righting a Wrong

Friendship has looked different in different seasons of my life. At times, friendship has been hard to come by, but other times, the Lord has blessed me with close friends. During these seasons of abundance, my friendships seem to be forged through both our faith in the Lord and walking through similar circumstances.

In college, those circumstances were late nights studying in the library, balancing newfound independence with missing home, jumping from one social event to the next, heartaches and new relationships, and a love for fightin' Texas Aggie football. More recently, the circumstances have looked like sleepless nights rocking babies, sharing the monotony of making school lunches, difficulties in balancing being a wife, mother, friend, employee, and looking forward to our monthly girls' night. During one of these seasons of friendship, I had to quickly work to right a wrong.

After a few days of spending time as a group, I quickly realized one of our friends felt left out. I could sense something was off when

I was around her and felt unsettled as I thought about the events leading up to seeing her. I could hear the Lord gently urging me to work to make it right.

I'm not normally a big phone caller and definitely don't love confrontation, but I knew this couldn't wait. I called her number with shaky hands, breathed unsteadily as I listened to the ring, and stumbled over my words as she answered. I asked her how she was doing and truly listened as she explained why she was hurt. I apologized for the part I had played, asked how I could make it right, and let her know how much I loved her, valued her as a friend, and thanked God for bringing her into my life. As I hung up, I knew that while everything hadn't been completely settled, I had peace that I had done my part to right a wrong as quickly as I could, starting the process of reconciliation.

A favorite biblical example of righting a wrong (and obeying and acting quickly) is the story of Zacchaeus in Luke 19:1–10.

He was a short—I love that Scripture includes this detail—wealthy tax-collector in Jericho who had made his money essentially by defrauding and over-taxing the people in his area. Not exactly the most popular guy. But as Jesus passed through the town, Zacchaeus climbed a sycamore tree in an attempt to see Him. It was there Jesus saw Zacchaeus and told him He was coming to his house. Zacchaeus received Him joyfully and said this: "Behold, Lord, the half of my goods I give to the poor. And if I have defrauded anyone of anything, I restore it fourfold" (Luke 19:8b).

Did you catch what Zacchaeus called Him? Zacchaeus called Jesus "Lord," reflecting his heart change, and then immediately paid restitution, reflecting his life change. Jesus wants both our hearts and our lives.

In *Prevailing Prayer*, D. L. Moody wrote:

We may sing our hymns and psalms, and offer prayers, but they will be an abomination to God, unless we are willing to be thoroughly straightforward in our daily life. Nothing will give Christianity such a hold upon the world as to have God's believing people begin to act in this way. Zacchaeus had probably more influence in Jericho after he made restitution than any other man in it.[46]

Righting a wrong isn't just about "doing the right thing." It's about maintaining our gospel witness. When we humble ourselves enough to admit our faults and quickly work to make them right, we show those around us that God has not only changed our hearts, He's changed our lives.

If you know there's a wrong in your life you need to make right, don't wait! Act with urgency in this, too. God's work in your life is too important not to.

QUICK TO ACTION

Intentional, intermittent hurry is not the same as living a hurried life. Hopefully this chapter has helped you to understand biblical reasons for hurry and opened your eyes to areas you may be hurrying where you don't actually need to act with urgency. Central to all of it is abiding so closely with Christ that your heart and life are both aligned with His eternal purposes.

Here are a few areas to get you started.

ASK FOR DISCERNMENT

Start training yourself to "test everything; hold fast what is good" (1 Thess. 5:21). As you ask the Lord for discernment and seek to hold fast to the good, act urgently where the Lord leads. Remember, there is great wisdom and value in pairing hurry with discernment. Don't allow your circumstances or attitude to needlessly dictate your hurry.

SHARE THE GOSPEL TODAY

Ask God to give you opportunities to talk about Him. Know that the way you live out your life (both in the mundane and the difficult) around unbelievers can have an eternally significant impact. There will never be a better time than today to share the gospel. You aren't guaranteed tomorrow, so don't wait! Call a friend or family member the Lord has laid on your heart, get lunch with an unbelieving co-worker, or be bold enough to share with a stranger at the park. Jesus is worth it!

RIGHT A WRONG

Be quick to acknowledge your sins and shortcomings and work to make them right. If you know there's a wrong that you've needed to right and have put it off, today's the day to pursue reconciliation. Quickly do what needs to be done so you can maintain your gospel witness and model true humility and repentance.

Hurry itself isn't the problem. In fact, God tells us to act with urgency under the right circumstances. Align your heart and life with Him so you'll confidently know when to halt and when to hurry.

QUESTIONS FOR REFLECTION

1. *Do you typically make hasty and reactionary decisions, or do you take time to ask God for discernment and wisdom? What practices can you put into place to make wise decisions?*

2. *When was the last time you shared the gospel? Has the Lord laid someone on your heart you need to share with today?*

3. *Can you think of a time when you obeyed God even when you didn't fully understand? What was the result?*

VERSE TO MEMORIZE

Behold, now is the favorable time;
behold, now is the day of salvation.

—2 CORINTHIANS 6:2B

CHAPTER THIRTEEN

A DAY IN THE LIFE: CREATING A SCHEDULE THAT MAKES ROOM

Yet you do not know what tomorrow will bring.
What is your life? For you are a mist that appears
for a little time and then vanishes.

JAMES 4:14

When I was in college at Texas A&M University (whoop!), I, along with every other freshman communications major, had to take a business math class. Even as someone who loves English and writing, I always enjoyed the practicality of math and the hard lines of the problem being either right or wrong. However, in this particular class, we had a section on math theories, and everything I thought I knew about math came into question. All of a sudden, math was high level with no clear answers and only theories that may or may not be true. There was no practicality, no steps to follow, and no clear path to take. I hated it.

My prayer is that this topic of creating margin and living life unhurried doesn't feel like my business math class. I don't want you to close the back cover of this book and feel like you have no clear path on what an unhurried life looks like in practice. I love plans (in case you hadn't picked up on that yet), and hopefully, this chapter serves as a planning guide for you that you can hold loosely with open hands, always seeking the Lord's purposes for your day first.

However, before jumping into some practical examples, I want to offer you a new perspective.

THE JEWISH DAY

Throughout recent years, I've enjoyed listening to a podcast called *Bema Discipleship*. In the first episode, "Trust the Story," host Marty Solomon walks through the creation account in Genesis 1. If you've read this chapter of Scripture at all, you may have noticed that after each day of creation, the text reads, "There was evening, and there was morning—the X day."[47]

Marty explains that even though listing the evening before morning in this refrain is a little strange to us, it would have made perfect sense to a Jewish audience because, unlike our day, the Jewish day begins at sunset. That in itself is interesting, but what he explained next truly shifted my perspective.

He explains that the Jewish day begins when the sun goes down as a reminder from God to His people that their day doesn't begin with production, it begins with rest.

Take a minute to let that sink in.

Marty even emphasized that this means their day doesn't begin with getting out of bed and thinking about everything that needs to be done that day. I don't know how your day begins, but mine is typically a mix of meeting the needs of my littles and looking at the calendar for the day. Often, the first few minutes are not restful—they are chaotic and overwhelming, and honestly, I just want to crawl back into bed some days.

If that's not enough, Marty takes it one step further. He explains that starting the day with rest is a reminder that our identity doesn't lie in what we do, but in who God created us to be. Our rate or level of production has little value to God who created us in His image.

I love this and pray that it shifts your perspective as it did mine.

Using this perspective and keeping in mind all we've learned about hurry and surrender up until this point, let's take a look at a few practical examples of a day designed with margin.

PRACTICALLY SPEAKING

Remember how I said I wanted to give you concrete examples and plans of what it looks like to create margin and live unhurried? As I spent time trying to figure out how to do that best, God so graciously reminded me He has made us each different and has laid different paths before us. The time commitments and mindset you have toward your day may be completely different than mine. However, the need to slow down and be in tune with the Spirit's leading is a command to all believers (John 16:13), no matter life stage, mindset, or amount of "free" time.

Below you will find three categories with examples and strategies for creating margin—you work full-time; you stay at home; you're somewhere in-between. However, know these are not meant to put you in a box. In fact, you might relate to more than one of these. Instead, these groupings are designed to help you practically see what an unhurried life may look like.

1. You Work Full-Time

After graduating college, I took the traditional route and jumped straight into a nine-to-five. That season of life was one of the most structured, routine, and laid out as far as what my day-to-day looked like. I knew exactly what time my alarm clock would go off each day (and let's be real, how many times I would hit snooze), what time I would eat lunch, and what time I would get home. My days were predictable and full.

Nobody tells you how exhausting working full-time is. I remember coming home as a newlywed to our 600-square-foot apartment and desperately trying to find the energy to make dinner for my new husband, but instead, calling for a pizza because it all felt like too much, and that's okay.

If this is currently your life stage, how can you live an unhurried life when structure reigns supreme? How can you overcome exhaustion to create margin for the Lord to work through you? What does this actually look like?

Here are a few practical tips and areas to focus on:

USE YOUR SCHEDULE TO SET A SPIRITUAL SCHEDULE

Yes, you are locked into a schedule. You can't just not show up for work when you're scheduled to be there. However, because you know this, you can work around and within that pre-existing schedule.

Ensure that you aren't hurrying out the door every morning but waking up in time to spend time with the Lord like David (Ps. 5:3), Jesus (Mark 1:35), Hannah (1 Sam. 1:19), and so many other followers of God. Then, use the breaks you do have strategically and intentionally.

CREATE OPPORTUNITIES WITHIN YOUR SCHEDULE

While a schedule can feel binding, it can actually be a tool you use for the kingdom. Create opportunities for the Lord to use you by heading to the same coffee shop each morning or going on a walk around your neighborhood at the same time every day. Make intentional conversation with coworkers and build relationships with the people that you spend so much of your time with.

MAXIMIZE TIME OFF

No matter what you do, working forty-plus hours a week is exhausting. If you're tempted to use those precious hours off to do little more than sit on the couch, you're not alone. However, a focused disciple of Jesus will work to maximize that time to engage with the Lord. This doesn't mean you never turn the TV on, but it does mean that you create that margin to spend time with the Lord, serve your neighbor, connect with other believers, and rest in Him.

BE AWARE OF THE CHALLENGES

In order to overcome the challenges associated with living an unhurried life as someone who works full-time, you must first be aware of those challenges. Here are a few to watch out for as you work to create margin: lack of flexibility, exhaustion, sameness and routine, idleness apart from work, misplaced priorities.

2. You Stay at Home

I entered the stay-at-home world right before my second son was born. All of a sudden, my schedule was fully dictated by what I wanted to do and what my children needed from me. I didn't have a boss telling me what time to show up to an office building or a professor who closed the classroom doors at a certain time. My schedule had become my own, and in many ways, I had no idea what to do with it.

Whether you are a stay-at-home parent, you are in between jobs, you're retired, or something else altogether, this season of life can feel ironically hurried. While you may have more time on your hands than ever before, this doesn't necessarily mean you're less busy.

So as someone with the power to say yes and no to the demands on your time, how are you going to make wise decisions to remain unhurried in this season? What does this practically look like for you?

Plan to Have No Plans

As a planner, I always joke that as long as my plan is to not have a plan, I can handle the unscheduled time. When it comes to living unhurried, not having a plan is one of the easiest ways to make yourself open, available, and in tune with the Spirit's promptings. For example, plan to sit in your front yard to let your kids play (remember the porch swing?). Or plan to take a leisurely walk around your school or a nearby park. Then as you do, pray as the Lord directs you and ask Him to provide opportunities to love, share with, and serve those He puts in your path. This is living unhurried.

Be Discerning with Your Schedule

During this season of life, it's easy to get into a pattern of saying yes. Yes to another Bible study, yes to volunteering, yes to helping out your friends, and yes to miscellaneous jobs. However, someone who is focused on the Lord's will above their own will ask the Lord when to say yes and when to say no. Sometimes this may mean saying no to coordinating the small group event and yes to dinner with the lost couple who goes to your gym. It may not always make sense in the world's eyes, but God's purposes are much bigger than this world. Ask the Lord to give you discernment so you can wisely choose when to commit and when to remain flexible.

USE YOUR TIME WISELY

In Ecclesiastes 1:2, Solomon in all of his wisdom says that "everything is meaningless." While this can feel like he's a real Derwood-downer, the reality is that he recognized that only what impacts eternity truly matters. Work to use the time and flexibility you've been given in this season to focus on eternal things. Fill your schedule by making time for the Lord and for the things He leads you towards. The other things are meaningless from an eternally significant perspective anyway.

BE ON GUARD

In many ways, the challenges of living an unhurried life while you stay at home are just the opposite of those for someone who works full-time. Satan takes good things and manipulates them, so be on guard and know what to look for during this season: too much unscheduled time; focus on temporal things; demands for your time that aren't God's will for you in this season

3. You're Somewhere In-Between (*running a side business, working part-time, volunteering, caregiving*)

For several years now I've been the co-founder of a content marketing business. If you had asked me if my plans were ever to "have my own business," I would've quickly said no and carried on about my day. However, as we've seen over and over, often the Lord has different plans.

On a crisp fall morning in October over a freshly brewed cup of coffee and a bagel with strawberry cream cheese, my

When your plate becomes (more) full and life gets crazy, it's here where margin seems to disappear.

friend proposed the idea of starting a business together. We both had young children so the idea of making money while maintaining a flexible schedule was appealing. We had similar communications backgrounds and contacts within the industry, and we knew there would be little to no upfront costs. It seemed like a win-win. And, for the most part, it has been.

However, when your plate becomes (more) full and life gets crazy, it's here where margin seems to disappear. The question becomes how do you balance it all in a way that honors and glorifies the Lord? In my case, it was how could I be a full-time mom, an entrepreneur, a wife, a small group director, and a million other titles all at the same time.

Whether you are spinning similar plates or your roles look totally different but are just as plentiful, here are a few practical tips for creating margin when your life is quite literally all over the place.

Prioritize What Matters

When looking at your day, what is really important? I don't mean the big meeting with the potential new client or your child's first game of the season; I mean what is truly important when it comes to eternity.

I love the story found in Luke 2:41–52 where twelve-year-old Jesus is sitting in the temple listening and learning from the teachers while His parents travel back home from Jerusalem. Jesus knew what was important. He recognized there was an eternal benefit to spending time learning, asking questions, and dwelling in His Father's house. However, His parents had an agenda He didn't follow, and as a result, Jesus was questioned by His mother. She had missed what was important.

When your schedule changes constantly, prioritizing is crucial. Pray that the meeting with the new client leads to gospel conversations, remember that your child's first game is an opportunity for encouragement and discipleship. Keeping eternal perspective throughout your day will help to keep priorities in line.

USE FLEXIBILITY AS AN ADVANTAGE

In this season of working and resting, commitments and free time, packed days and empty calendars, recognize that the flexibility can actually be a benefit. Let go of the tendency to make every day look like the previous one. Work early in the morning one day and during your child's nap time the next. Let that be okay. However, in all of the flexibility, remember God never changes. He wants to be in your early mornings, your quiet afternoons, and your jam-packed evenings. Don't let the flexibility become spiritual stagnation.

REMOVE THE DISTRACTIONS

While it may not be realistic to remove all distractions (e.g., kids running around, the need to have some sort of income), it is realistic to remove what is distracting you from creating the margin you need in your life. This might mean saying no to the extra volunteer activity. Or cutting out a class or activity that you only semi-enjoy. Even if it feels like you should say yes, really seek the Lord and ask if He's calling you to say no instead.

REMAIN VIGILANT

Finally, as someone in this "all over the place" stage of life, it's imperative that you're aware of the challenges you face in order to combat them as they come your way. Be on guard for: focusing on so much that you're not focused on any one thing at all; filling your schedule for the sake of busyness; over-prioritizing the temporal things in your life; failing to make the most of your flexibility.

No matter which category you may currently fall into, the bottom line remains the same for us all: God wants every piece of us. He wants our hearts and minds. He wants our gifts and resources. And He wants each minute of every day. Why? His eternal purposes are good and so much greater than we can even hope or imagine. What choices and decisions are you (or could you be) making to develop a lifestyle more surrendered to Him?

In *The Rest of God*, Mark Buchanan writes,

> I cannot think of a single advantage I've ever gained from being in a hurry. But a thousand broken and missed things, tens of thousands, lie in the wake of all the rushing. . . . Through all that haste I thought I was making up time. It turns out I was throwing it away.[48]

We only have so much time. James reminds us in James 4:14b, "For you are a mist that appears for a little time and then vanishes."

In certain stages of life, it may seem like hurry and busyness are the key to doing more, making up time, and "succeeding." But the truth is, if the posture of your heart is more self-focused rather than surrendered to Jesus, then your rushing is merely throwing what little time you have away. Don't waste the time and opportunities you've been given! You are in this season of life for a reason, so seek His purposes day by day.

QUESTIONS FOR REFLECTION

1. *How does your day typically begin? What changes do you need to make to shift your perspective from what you need to do to who God created you to be?*

2. *Which life-stage above do you relate with the most (you work full time, you stay at home, you're somewhere in-between)? What is the biggest challenge you have in creating margin in this season?*

3. *How are you striving to live your life daily surrendered to Him? Remember, we are all works in progress. Prayerfully consider putting into practice the things God is showing you through this journey over the coming days and see what transformations He will bring about through your obedience.*

VERSE TO MEMORIZE

Yet you do not know what tomorrow will bring. What is your life? For you are a mist that appears for a little time and then vanishes.

—JAMES 4:14

CHAPTER FOURTEEN

GRACE UPON GRACE: WHAT HAPPENS IF I START TO HURRY AGAIN?

But he said to me, "My grace is sufficient for you, for my power is made perfect in weakness." Therefore I will boast all the more gladly of my weaknesses, so that the power of Christ may rest upon me. For the sake of Christ, then, I am content with weaknesses, insults, hardships, persecutions, and calamities. For when I am weak, then I am strong.

2 CORINTHIANS 12:9–10

I could sense the tension rising in my mom. Even as a pre-teen, I could perceive when that line between calm and controlled to frustrated and snappy started to blur ... and I knew it wouldn't be pretty for anyone.

My brother, who is nearly seven years younger than me, had been in rare form. Not only was he demanding things to be his way, but he was doing so in the most annoying, high-pitched voice. It was the kind that makes your skin crawl after just a couple of sentences.

As he went on and on, I knew the snap was coming. Sure enough, with the perfect mom death stare activated, my mom lectured my brother, who promptly stopped listening long enough to say this (in his best whiny voice):

"But whining is the only way I get what I want!"

The truth is, he wasn't completely wrong. His perfected, skin-crawling whiny voice was horrible enough to make pretty much anyone give him what he wanted just to make it stop. Thankfully, my parents didn't give in to his whines, and with discipline, he did eventually grow out of this. Now, ironically, my brother has one of the deepest voices I know.

I think his whine-laden words have stuck with me all these years because, so often, they're true of my life, too. The minute things stop going my way, I revert back to my sinful tendencies. I think, "But doing _____ is the only way I get what I want!" It may not be whining (though sometimes it is). Instead, it may be the way I start to hurry again, the way I try to start manipulating and controlling situations, or the way I put my desires above the needs of others. However, at the heart of it all, it's the way I stop following the leading of the Spirit and instead choose to give into my flesh.

What about you? Is there a sinful tendency you regularly go back to when life starts to get a little out of hand? Do you feel as if it's the fastest and easiest way to truly get what you want?

As I've studied and learned about the importance of slowing down and creating margin, there's been a lingering question that's plagued me: What happens if I start to hurry again?

But there's a second, even more important question that follows: Do I truly believe God's grace is enough? Grace is commonly defined as the unmerited favor of God toward us, and it is the foundation of the gospel.

It's here, in this reality of grace upon grace, that the Lord has given peace, assurance, and a sense of completion. We're not alone. Once again, Scripture is our guide as we study examples of people who also struggled with this return to old ways.

I DO WHAT I DO NOT WANT

If there's anyone in the Bible who had to completely turn from his old ways to pursue the things of God, it was Paul. He went from relentlessly persecuting Christians to becoming one of the boldest believers in all of history. However, he gives us insight into this battle between his old and new ways in Romans 7.

Paul writes to believers in Rome about the relationship between sin and the law, and as he does, he expresses the tension between following Jesus and living in the flesh. He writes:

"For I do not understand my own actions. For I do not do what I want, but I do the very thing I hate. . . . For I know that nothing good dwells in me, that is, in my flesh. For I have the desire to do what is right, but not the ability to carry it out. For I do not do the good I want, but the evil I do not want is what I keep on doing" (Rom. 7:15, 18–19).

> How often do you start your day with the best of intentions only to be derailed by something not in your plan?

You can almost hear the desperation and frustration in his voice. He wants to do what is good and right and pleasing to the Lord, and yet doesn't have the ability to carry it out. Instead, he gives in to those sinful tendencies, repeatedly caught in this chasm between living a godly life and walking in the way of the world.

Can you relate? How often do you start your day with the best of intentions only to be derailed by something not in your plan? Or do you ever find yourself falling back into the same negative thought patterns or lifestyle habits that you've worked so hard to change?

The good news is Paul doesn't stop at this tension. Here's the hope he offers: "Wretched man that I am! Who will deliver me from this body of death? Thanks be to God through Jesus Christ our Lord!" (Rom. 7:24–25a).

Don't miss this! Yes, we are wretched. Yes, we will continue to daily and even hourly battle our flesh. And yes, the bodies we are living in are bodies of death. But we have a Deliverer. The blood of Jesus is enough, and His grace covers even our most stubborn sins!

This is the truth we must remember when the pace of our lives speeds up, when we fail to create margin, and when our plans start to take priority in our hearts. Stop and repent, knowing His grace covers this, too!

Be honest with the Lord. Pursue intimacy with Him. It's much easier to surrender your will to His when you start by honestly telling Him what your will, desires, and plans are.

Like Paul, we must keep waging war. We must keep disciplining ourselves to keep our flesh under control (1 Cor. 9:27). It's the "how" we must figure out.

TAKE IT BACK TO THE BASICS

I grew up playing sports, and while I'm clearly not a professional athlete these days, the fundamentals I learned stuck with me. There are countless sports stories and illustrations I could reference, but most of them come back to the same point: in order to play a game well, you must master the basics. A basketball player would lose the game if he couldn't shoot the basketball. A runner jumping hurdles would trip every time if she didn't have the right form. A baseball player would strike out if he didn't know how to swing a bat. The basics matter.

When it comes to waging spiritual war against our flesh, we too must return again and again to the basics. Here are a few fundamentals.

Be Aware of Sin Tendencies

This world is broken. If you've turned the TV on or scrolled social media for even a few minutes in recent days, you can probably recount awful, evil, heart-wrenching stories of this world's brokenness. However, the truth is, if we take a few minutes to examine our own hearts, we will find the same brokenness and sin patterns there too.

For example, when we knowingly choose to prioritize our plans over the Lord's purposes, we pave a pathway for sin. When we fail to create margin in our lives and tune out the Spirit's leading, we create opportunities for sin. When we rush around blind to everything but our own to-do lists, we are flirting on the edge of disobedience and sin.

Some days the weight of it all feels overwhelming.

In Romans 8, Paul writes that "the whole creation has been groaning together in the pains of childbirth until now" (Rom. 8:22b). He explains how we have hope in Christ and wait eagerly for His return, but in the meantime, we suffer and groan as both internal and external brokenness avails. While we remain in this body of flesh, there will be an ongoing tension between the flesh and the Spirit. As a result, we long for relief and freedom; the redemption of our bodies from the temptations of the world (Rom. 8:23).

So what should we do? How do we respond?

We could choose bitterness, callousness, anger, fear, frustration, and sorrow. Or we could obey the truth of Scripture and repent and lament.

Repent

"Or do you have no regard for the wealth of His kindness and tolerance and patience [in withholding His wrath]? Are you [actually] unaware or ignorant [of the fact] that God's kindness leads you to repentance [that is, to **change your inner self, your old way of thinking—seek His purpose for your life**]?" (Rom. 2:4 AMP).

We serve a good, kind, and patient God. He is one who can take the brokenness and make it whole. But Paul reminded the church in Romans that their response (and our response) to His kindness should be repentance. He also reminds the church at Corinth that it is godly sorrow that leads us to repentance (2 Cor. 7:10–11).

A recognition of our sin is not the same thing as the undue shame and guilt we put on ourselves in an effort to keep up; instead, it's an awareness of the things we do that break God's heart.

When we encounter the Spirit's conviction and experience godly sorrow, we repent by turning away from our sin and walking forward in obedience to Him. So when we start to hurry, we slow down. And when we start to ignore promptings from the Spirit, we stop, create margin, and listen intently.

Lament

In a *Desiring God* article, Pastor Mark Vroegop writes,

> Lament prayers take faith. Talking to God instead of getting sinfully angry or embittered requires biblical conviction. Laying out the messy struggles of your soul and then asking—again and again—for God to help you requires a solid theological mooring. **Laments turn toward God when sorrow tempts you to run from him** (emphasis added).[49]

Lament is a passionate expression of grief or sorrow. It's a mourning and deep grief over something. As believers, our lament is a prayer to the only One who has power over the brokenness and who is able to comfort us in our grief. Why and how do we lament well?

WHY DO WE LAMENT?

To mourn the brokenness (Matt. 5:4, James 4:9)

It's okay to be upset over the state of the world and/or the state of our hearts. Bring it to the Lord.

To ask for help

This is a simple admission: "God, we need You." He alone can give us the help and healing we need.

To display our trust in God's sovereignty

We know the ending. The tomb is empty, Jesus has risen, and He is coming again. Until then, our lament displays the confidence we have in His plan. It is a waiting and a longing for the Lord to come and make things right; to make the broken whole again.

HOW DO WE LEARN TO LAMENT?

Lament takes practice. Here are a few ways to get started:

Ask the Lord to break your heart for what breaks His: If we are going to lament, we must avoid callousness. It's not easy or painless or fun, but true lament requires us to see the world through God's eyes.

Read the Psalms: The Psalms are full of laments and songs of sorrow. If you're looking for good ones to start with, read Psalms 7, 13, 38, and 130.

Practice: Finally, just start. Come before the Lord passionately bringing your sorrow to Him.

When we experience brokenness, we can choose to react emotionally, or we can choose to respond biblically—repent and lament the sin within us and around us. What will you do?

ACCEPT GOD'S GRACE

Another thing we tend to forget when we are hurried is the importance of accepting and appropriating the grace God offers, believing it is enough. Enough to cover our weaknesses and propensities toward the things of the flesh. Enough to cover the prioritization of our wants and desires. Enough to cover our fears of not getting it all done or meeting our own (or others') expectations. Enough to cover our hurry!

Ephesians 2:8–9 says, "For by grace you have been saved through faith. And this is not your own doing; it is the gift of God, not a result of works, so that no one may boast."

We wait patiently, asking God to refine our character.

Our salvation is by grace and through faith. When we give into temptation and return to our sinful tendencies, this is the truth we must return to. And if we preach this to ourselves, we must also teach our hearts to believe that this same grace God offers is sufficient. This means we don't have to believe *and* make up for it with good works or religious living or self-inflicted punishment. It means we walk forward in the freedom Christ offers through His grace.

Appropriating this grace means we step forward in faith to take hold of what is ours in Christ. It's a lifestyle involving the steadfast pursuit of God and the reliance on His strength in our weakness. It involves humbly submitting to God's providential work in our lives. And often, it means we wait patiently, asking God to refine our character, that which we have faithfully appropriated in Christ.

Paul knew this truth well and explained it to the church in Corinth. After the Lord gave Paul "a thorn in his flesh" (as a side note, we aren't sure exactly what this was, but it doesn't sound pleasant) to keep him from becoming conceited, this is what God told him.

But he said to me, "My grace is sufficient for you, for my power is made perfect in weakness." Therefore I will boast all the more gladly of my weaknesses, so that the power of Christ may rest upon me. For the sake of Christ, then, I am content with weaknesses, insults, hardships, persecutions, and calamities. For when I am weak, then I am strong. (2 Cor. 12:9–10)

Did you catch that? His grace is sufficient. Our weaknesses serve to put the grace God offers and desires for us to take hold of on display.

I recently had a conversation with a friend about wanting to display the whole gospel in my life . . . not a partial one, not just a pretty one, but the complete one. When I started writing this book and studying what it is to live a slow, surrendered life, I somewhat naively hoped to reach a finish line. But the reality is, I am still a work in progress. I still rush around blind to the needs of others, I still hurry in an attempt to do and be more, and I still fail to create daily margin. But I have also experienced the joy of surrender and the peace that comes with following His promptings. Where I am weak, He is strong. His grace is enough for me.

What does this mean for our planning, perfectionism, hurry, and striving? It means we, again and again, lay them at the feet of Jesus, choose to believe His grace is sufficient, and give Him glory because it is.

DO THE WORK

One last foundation to return to is active, ongoing obedience. Recall that we talked about sanctification earlier.

Near the end of David's life, he starts the preparations for the building of the temple. God told David that he wouldn't be the one to build it, but instead, his son Solomon would have peace in his time so he could build the temple. In all of David's planning, we get a little glimpse into what he tells his son in 1 Chronicles 28:9 (NIV).

> "And you, my son Solomon, acknowledge the God of your father, and serve him with wholehearted devotion and with a willing mind, for the LORD searches every heart and understands every desire and every thought. If you seek him, he will be found by you; but if you forsake him, he will reject you forever. Consider now, for the LORD has chosen you to build a house as the sanctuary. Be strong and **do the work.**"

It boils down to a single command: "Do the work."

David didn't say, "if you feel like it" or "when it's convenient"; he commanded his son to obey the Lord's purpose for his life. And for Solomon, this meant building a temple.

What does it mean for you? What is God's specific purpose and calling for you during this season? No matter what it is, it requires a wholehearted genuine surrender of your plans, feelings, and desires in favor of God's purposes. It takes strength, focus, discipline, and determination, but the eternal reward will be sweet, and the fellowship with the Spirit will bring joy and peace.

How do we do this? Step by step, day by day, minute by minute we die to self (1 Cor. 15:31b). We lay down our selfish motives, agendas, and desires, and listen to the Spirit's promptings. Then, when He speaks, we quickly say, "Yes, Lord!" and get to work.

"SLOW DOWN AGAIN"

Do you remember how this book started? It started with chaos and hurry and a walk to my mailbox where my sweet neighbor exclaimed, "I don't know how you do it all!" And do you remember how that night the Lord called me to "give careful thought to my ways" (Hag. 1:5–6)?

Since then, I've heard the Lord gently whisper to my heart and mind over and over and over . . . "*Samantha, slow down again.*" Oh, how deep His love is for me! He doesn't stop pursuing and doesn't stop reminding me that His ways are always better. I don't have to do it all! I don't have to rush through life trying to accomplish more, control more, do more . . . and neither do you.

For the perfectionist trying to be perfect, the control freak trying to control, and the do-it-all go-getter who is always working to do more . . . it is finished (John 19:30). He has done it all! He alone is perfect, He alone is in control, and He alone has done enough to pave the way for us to be with Him.

Do you believe it though? In your heart and mind and depth of your spirit? Do you believe that His grace is sufficient for you? And do you strive to live it out, even when the battle to daily surrender is fierce and full of hardship?

Until we experience freedom from this broken world either through death or Jesus' return, this will be something we fight over and over again. Thankfully in Christ, we are ultimately victorious. Although we struggle with legalism, perfectionism, and our flesh, Scripture tells us we are no longer to be controlled by sin's power (Rom. 6:6). Abundant grace is found in Christ alone. His is the victory!

When you start to hurry, when you prioritize your plans over His purposes yet again, and when you fail to create margin in your life, humbly kneel before Him. He offers forgiveness and grace sufficient for today. Not only that, but His embrace is tender, and His voice is full of love as He gently whispers, "Slow down again."

QUESTIONS FOR REFLECTION

1. *Can you identify a pattern, behavior, or habit in your life you go back to over and over again in an attempt "to get what you want" (remember the whining story)? Have you spent time repenting and lamenting this?*

2. *Do you truly believe God's grace is enough to cover every weakness, temptation, and even deliberate sin in your life? What does it look like to walk forward in this grace?*

3. *What practices and disciplines can you put into place to help you "slow down again" when you hear the Spirit's gentle promptings?*

VERSE TO MEMORIZE

*But he said to me, "My grace is sufficient for you,
for my power is made perfect in weakness." Therefore I will
boast all the more gladly of my weaknesses, so that
the power of Christ may rest upon me.*

—2 CORINTHIANS 12:9

EPILOGUE

Three years after building the porch swing, my husband built a beautiful window seat surrounded by built-in bookshelves in our front office. We painted the shelves a muted blue and covered the seat in a textured grey fabric. I added some coordinating pillows, but also spent over a month crocheting a granny square pillow cover to add to the seat as decoration (sounds like slowing down, right?)!

However, as I sit here on this window seat watching birds fly in and out of our slowly budding crepe myrtle, I'm dwelling on the reality that I will never finish living out the words of this book.

When God prompted me to "consider my ways" and called me to start writing years ago, I think in the back of my mind, I hoped to arrive somewhere. I wanted to arrive at unhurry. To arrive at a fully Spirit-led life. To arrive at surrendering control. In some ways I hoped to be an "expert" and to confidently model how to live unhurried.

Here's the truth though: Just last week we were the family walking ten minutes late into church, tired, frustrated, and honestly just amazed that we made it. I'm eight months pregnant with baby number four and the reality is, I'm moving slower and couldn't find an outfit that fit like I wanted. On top of that, the older two boys spent the morning going from happily play-wrestling to actually throwing punches in matters of seconds, the toddler demanded to get in the bath and then out of the bath and then in the bath with meltdowns in-between, and my husband was putting in a little last-minute studying for the lesson he was teaching that morning. It wasn't peaceful, it wasn't intentional, and it wasn't slow.

From the beginning, I prayed that the Lord would use this book and these words to draw even one person closer to Him. If you're reading these words, I'm humbled and grateful and in awe and praying that's you . . . but, it's also me.

I clearly haven't "arrived." I'm not the perfect picture of unhurried. But I am closer to God than I was.

As I sat in church that morning, our pastor read about the potter and the clay in Jeremiah 18. Jeremiah watched the potter skillfully craft the clay, and then rework it into something else, "as it seemed good to the potter to do" (Jer. 18:4). Our pastor explained how we are like the clay in the potter's hands. He then led the congregation in singing these words:

> Have thine own way, Lord!
> Have thine own way!
> Thou art the potter,
> I am the clay.
> Mold me and make me
> after thy will,
> while I am waiting,
> yielded and still.[50]

"Yielded and still." I sang these words and realized that, over and over, this has been and will be my prayer. I want to yield to the Lord's will for my life, and I desperately pray that you do, too. While we are on this earth, it will never come naturally, but as we've seen, it will always be worth pursuing.

Together, let's choose to slow down again. To create margin again. To surrender control again.

Have Thine own way in me, Lord!

INDICATORS OF THE FRUIT OF THE SPIRIT IN YOUR LIFE

S kim through this now (I'm actually giving you permission), but come back, spend time reading the Scripture references listed, and let some of it soak in later:

Indicators of Love

- You measure your actions, thoughts, and decisions against the Word of God. Love is not conditional, temporary, or optional. If we bear the fruit of love, we will strive to practice it in our hearts, souls, and minds at all times (Matt. 22:37, 1 Cor. 16:14).

- You go out of your way to serve everyone . . . not just the people who are easy to love (Matt. 5:44, Luke 6:32).

- Your actions line up with your talk (1 John 3:18).

- You hate the things that displease and dishonor God (Amos 5:15a, Rom. 12:9).

- You think of others before yourself. Love is both selfless and sacrificial (Matt. 22:39b, John 15:13, Rom. 13:10).

Indicators of Joy

- Your circumstances don't define you. True joy does not come and go; instead, joy is rooted in the hope found in Christ alone (Neh. 8:10, John 16:22).

- Trials strengthen your faith (Ps. 30:5, James 1:2).

- You eagerly seek time with the Lord now and anticipate His coming (Hab. 3:18, Rom. 15:13).

- You pursue the unity of the church. This means you are present, serving, loving, and encouraging your fellow believers (Phil. 2:2).

Indicators of Peace

- You keep your heart and mind focused on the Lord (Isa. 26:3, Col. 3:15).

- You avoid unrighteous conflict and seek to live in harmony (Isa. 32:17, Heb. 12:14).

- Even in chaos, you are calm. You trust the One who stills the storm (Mark 4:39, 1 Cor. 14:33).

- Your heart is light. You don't constantly bear the burden of fear and anxiety (John 14:27, Phil. 4:6–7).

- You are confident in your relationship with God because you know what Jesus did for you (Rom. 5:1, Eph. 2:14).

Indicators of Patience

- You accept that growth takes time and are willing to do the work, day by day (Luke 8:15).

- You work to fulfill your calling by genuinely loving and caring for those around you (Eph. 4:1–2, 1 Cor. 13:4, 1 Thess. 5:14).

- You know trials are temporary, so you endure with hope, knowing Jesus is coming again (Rom. 12:12, James 5:7–8).
- You believe that it's not too late for anyone to be saved (1 Tim. 1:16, 2 Peter 3:9).

Indicators of Kindness

- Your words and actions are an extension of God's kindness that leads others to repentance and salvation (Rom. 2:4).
- You see the needs and hurts of others and do what you can to help. The kind person speaks words of life and encouragement to others (Zech. 7:9–10).
- Your kindness is contagious. It challenges and teaches others to follow your example (Prov. 31:26, 2 Tim. 2:24–25a).
- When others are cruel, you are kind, imitating the kindness and forgiveness God shows us (Luke 6:35, Eph. 4:32).

Indicators of Goodness

- You are aware of your deep need for the only One who is truly good. We can only bear the fruit of goodness because of salvation in Jesus and His work in our lives (Titus 3:4–5, Ps. 86:5).
- Laziness, weariness, and/or busyness do not keep you from doing the right thing (Gal. 6:9–10, Mic. 6:8).
- You regularly ask the Lord for wisdom. You are able to rightly discern between good and evil (Isa. 5:20, 1 Tim. 4:4a).
- Your goodness is not contingent on the actions and attitudes of those around you. Goodness is a heart issue (Luke 6:27–28, 45).

Indicators of Faithfulness

- Your life is steady, consistent, and focused on eternity. You cling to the promises of God (Prov. 20:6, 1 Thess. 5:24).

- You know even small responsibilities and stewardships matter (Luke 16:10, Rom. 1:17).

- You consistently tell others about God's faithfulness to you (Ps. 89:1, Lam. 3:22– 23).

- You stand firm when troubles come. You refuse to abandon the ways of the Lord. Faithfulness is believing God is who He says He is and remaining steadfast in your belief despite the uncertainties of life (Prov. 3:3, 2 Cor. 5:6–7).

- Your prayer life reflects your beliefs about God. You ask big things because you know He is able (Matt. 17:20, Heb. 11:1).

Indicators of Gentleness

- You seek comfort and rest in the arms of Jesus—the One who is available and ready to take your burdens (Matt. 11:28–30).

- You combat the severity and harshness of the world with a meek and humble spirit, desiring all to be saved (2 Tim. 2:24–25).

- When a brother or sister in Christ is caught in sin, you seek to restore them, knowing you, too, are vulnerable to sin (Gal. 6:1).

- You know your calling and your value. You display characteristics that are pleasing to God (Eph. 4:1–2, 1 Peter 3:4).

Indicators of Self-Control

- Your perspective is eternal; regularly training your flesh to yield its desires to the things of the Lord. The self-controlled person lives with the end in mind (1 Cor. 9:25–27a, 1 Peter 4:7).

- You don't respond to offense and hardship with anger. You don't willingly yield your peace to anyone or anything (Prov. 25:28, James 1:19–20).

- You rely on the Holy Spirit within you—not your own feelings, emotions, or reactions (2 Tim. 1:7).

- You intentionally train, mentor, and disciple those coming behind you. Your life is worth imitating (Titus 2:3b–6, 1 Cor. 11:1).

ACKNOWLEDGMENTS

The words in this book are not only a reflection of the Lord's work in my life, but also evidence of the many people who have come alongside me. You have each urged me to be "steadfast, immovable, always abounding in the work of the Lord, knowing that in the Lord your labor is not in vain" (1 Cor. 15:58). I'm grateful!

To my husband, Dustin, you are evidence of the Lord's goodness and generosity to me. Thank you for leading, encouraging, and loving me day by day. The countless hours you've entertained children so I could write, spurring me on when I didn't know if should keep going and making me laugh in the middle of it all, haven't gone unseen. And to my children, Eli, Caden, Hudson, and Charlie, my prayer is that one day, these words help you to know and love Jesus more. I love y'all!

Mom and Dad, you introduced me to Jesus and have taught me what it looks like to follow Him in seasons of goodness and seasons of sorrow. Your unconditional love and selflessness have shaped who I am in Christ, and I'm thankful.

Abbey, nobody sees me, knows me, and loves me like Jesus more than you. Thank you for celebrating my victories, feeling my struggles (probably even more deeply than I do), and speaking truth to my doubts. Your life reflects Jesus, and I want to be more like Him because of you. Zach, thank you for your encouragement, prayers, and steadfast presence. Thank you both for believing in this book before I did! And to my family, immediate and extended, the Lord has blessed me by giving me each of you. Many of these words are a result of the love you've shown me.

Paula Vawter, your wisdom and encouragement to "soften it a little" are woven all throughout this book. There are few women who have poured into me, charged me with scriptural integrity, and taught me how to live a life "poured out" more than you (Phil. 2:17). Thank you for teaching, editing, encouraging, and spending countless hours in your living room discipling me. It's an honor and joy to imitate you as you imitate Christ (1 Cor. 11:1).

To the women who offered honest feedback, spurred me on, and did the hard work of editing a 200-page Word document, thank you for helping to shape this book and point me to Jesus along the way. Candace Cofer, Kaitlin Dees, Maribeth Fisher, Liz Graham, Samantha Hanni, Kelly King, Lisa Melton, and Shandyn Paul, I'm so grateful for you!

To my acquisitions editors, Judy Dunagan and Erin Davis, and my developmental editor, Pam Pugh, I'm so thankful for your partnership in the spread of the gospel. Thank you for using your gifts and guiding me with your expertise. This book is only what it is because of each of you.

To the incredible team at Moody Publishers, including Christianne Debysingh, Hope Francis, Joyce Li, Kaylee Lockenour, Trillia Newbell, Connor Sterchi, and Ashley Torres, and the team at Compel Training, including Tracie Miles, thank you for investing in me. This open door was an answer to countless prayers, and I continue to be humbled and in awe of how God used you to provide. And to Riley Moody, the cover exceeded my expectations. Thank you for giving an image to my words.

To my home church, Quail Springs Baptist Church, it's a joy to be a part of Christ's body with you. I'm grateful for the women in my discipleship groups, friends in connect groups, and countless leaders who have walked alongside me in the pursuit of godliness. I love you all.

Jesus, be glorified in the words on these pages. You alone are worthy of praise!

"Now to him who is able to do far more abundantly than all that we ask or think, according to the power at work within us, to him be glory in the church and in Christ Jesus throughout all generations, forever and ever. Amen" (Eph. 3:20–21).

NOTES

1. Ben Stuart, *Rest & War: Rhythms of a Well-Fought Life* (Nashville: Thomas Nelson, 2022), 145.
2. I wrote about this incident at https://www.samanthadeckerwrites.com/blog/the-danger-of-doing-it-all.
3. Sam Paul, "American Families Barely Spend Quality Time Together," *New York Post*, March 20, 2018, https://nypost.com/2018/03/20/american-families-barely-spend-quality-time-together/.
4. "Be Thou My Vision," Hymnary.org, https://hymnary.org/text/be_thou_my_vision_o_lord_of_my_heart.
5. *Merriam-Webster.com Dictionary*, s.v. "margin," https://www.merriam-webster.com/dictionary/margin.
6. "1254. bara'," Bible Hub, accessed March 1, 2023, https://biblehub.com/hebrew/1254.htm.
7. I wrote about this busy time at https://www.risenmotherhood.com/articles/strains-of-the-season-parties.
8. John Piper, "What Is an Idol?," *Desiring God*, January 5, 2024, https://www.desiringgod.org/interviews/what-is-an-idol.
9. "Pastors Share Top Reasons They've Considered Quitting Ministry in the Past Year," Barna Group, April 27, 2022, https://www.barna.com/research/pastors-quitting-ministry/.
10. I wrote about memorizing Scripture at https://www.samanthadeckerwrites.com/blog/more-than-just-memorization.
11. C. S. Lewis, *Mere Christianity* (New York: HarperCollins, 2001), 74.

12. "Matthew 6:19–21," Spurgeon's Notes on Matthew, https://gracegems .org/32/amatthew.htm.

13. Dwayne Milioni, *A New Baptist Catechism: Important Questions and Answers to Instruct Children about God and the Gospel* (Timmonsville, SC: Seed Publishing Group, 2020), 21.

14. Bill Gaither and Gloria Gaither, "Because He Lives," 1969, https:// namethathymn.com/christian-hymns/because-he-lives-lyrics.html.

15. Kelly Minter, "Your Kingdom Come," in *When You Pray: A Study of Six Prayers in the Bible* (Brentwood, TN: Lifeway Press, 2023), 30.

16. John Piper, "The Sovereignty of God: 'I Will Accomplish All My Purpose,'" *Desiring God*, March 10, 2023, https://www.desiringgod. org/messages/the-sovereignty-of-god-my-counsel-shall-stand-and-i-will-accomplish-all-my-purpose.

17. Jerry Bridges, *Trusting God* (Colorado Springs: NavPress, 2016), 60.

18. "G3306 - Menō - Strong's Greek Lexicon (kjv)," Blue Letter Bible, accessed June 9, 2023, https://www.blueletterbible.org/lexicon/g3306/ kjv/tr/0-1/.

19. "Hudson Taylor: Abiding in Christ," Path2Prayer, https://www.path2 prayer.com/famous-christians-their-lives-and-writings-including-free-books/j-hudson-taylor-pioneer-missionary-to-china/hudson-taylor-abiding-in-christ.

20. Tara Dew, *Overflowing Joy: What Jesus Says About a Joy-Filled Life* (Nashville: B&H Books, 2024), 98.

21. Nancy Guthrie, *The One Year Praying Through the Bible for Your Kids* (Carol Stream, IL: Tyndale, 2016), 49.

22. C. S. Lewis, *The Lion, the Witch and the Wardrobe* (New York: Harper-Trophy, 2008).

23. I wrote about spiritual disciplines at https://www.samanthadecker writes.com/blog/lord-i-want-to-be-more-like-you.

24. For further study, I recommend *Spiritual Disciplines for the Christian Life* by Donald S. Whitney.

25. Ben Stuart, *Rest & War: The Rhythm of a Well-Fought Life* (New York: HarperCollins, 2022), 111.

26. Robert Robinson (1735–1790), "Come, Thou Fount of Every Blessing," Hymnary.org., https://hymnary.org/text/come_thou_fount_of_every_ blessing.

27. I wrote about the Israelites and manna at https://www.samanthadecker writes.com/blog/have-you-been-in-the-word-today.

28. I wrote about prayer at https://www.samanthadeckerwrites.com/blog/prayer-as-a-process.

29. I wrote about community at https://www.samanthadeckerwrites.com/blog/the-importance-of-biblical-community.

30. Oxford English Dictionary, "community."

31. "What Are Sunday Scaries?" The Sunday Scaries Podcast, http://www.sunday-scaries.com/what-are-sunday-scaries.

32. *Merriam-Webster.com Dictionary*, s.v. "busybody," https://www.merriam-webster.com/dictionary/busybody.

33. Paula created this content on a handout she used at a Bible study and gave me permission to use it.

34. "Strong's #5486, Old & New Testament Greek Lexical Dictionary," StudyLight.org, https://www.studylight.org/lexicons/eng/greek/5486.html.

35. "Strong's #5485, Old & New Testament Greek Lexical Dictionary," StudyLight.org, https://www.studylight.org/lexicons/eng/greek/5485.html.

36. Warren W. Wiersbe, *The Bible Exposition Commentary* (Wheaton, IL: Victor Books, 1996), 1:239.

37. Matthew McMullan, "Martin Luther King, Jr. on Work: 'Here Lived a Great Street Sweeper Who Swept His Job Well,'" Alliance for American Manufacturing, Janaury 18, 2019, https://www.american manufacturing.org/blog/martin-luther-king-jr-on-work-here-lived-a-great-street-sweeper-who-swept-his-job-well/.

38. Sharon Hodde Miller, *The Cost of Control: Why We Crave It, the Anxiety It Gives Us, and the Real Power God Promises* (Grand Rapids, MI: Baker, 2022), 38.

39. I wrote about seasons of life at https://www.samanthadeckerwrites.com/blog/pursuing-growth-in-every-spiritual-season.

40. "Joshua Fought the Battle of Jericho," Hymnary.org, https://hymnary.org/text/you_may_talk_about_the_men_of_gideon.

41. *VeggieTales*, episode 9, "Josh and the Big Wall!," directed by Chris Olsen and Phil Vischer, released November 18, 1997, https://www.imdb.com/title/tt0284607/.

42. Alan Carr, "How to Make Your Walls Fall Down Flat," The Sermon Notebook, http://www.sermonnotebook.org/joshua/Josh%206_1-21 .htm.

43. D. A. Carson, *For the Love of God: A Daily Companion for Discovering the Riches of God's Word* (Nottingham: Inter-Varsity Press, 2010), 23.

44. *Merriam-Webster.com Dictionary*, s.v. "discerning," https://www .merriam-webster.com/dictionary/discerning.

45. Carl F. H. Henry, *Grace Quotes*, December 11, 2019, https://gracequotes .org/author-quote/carl-f-h-henry/#bio.

46. D. L. Moody, *Prevailing Prayer* (Chicago: Moody Publishers [Moody Classics], 2016), 52.

47. Marty Solomon, host, *BEMA Discipleship*, season 1, episode 1, "Trust the Story," September 8, 2016, https://www.bemadiscipleship.com/1.

48. Mark Buchanan, *The Rest of God: Restoring Your Soul by Restoring Sabbath* (Nashville, TN: Thomas Nelson, 2007), 45.

49. Mark Vroegop, "Dare to Hope in God: How to Lament Well," *Desiring God*, April 6, 2019, https://www.desiringgod.org/articles/ dare-to-hope-in-god.

50. Adelaide A. Pollard, "Have Thine Own Way, Lord." Hymnary.org., https://hymnary.org/text/have_thine_own_way_lord.

You finished reading!

Did this book help you in some way? If so, please consider writing an honest review wherever you purchase your books. Your review gets this book into the hands of more readers and helps us continue to create biblically faithful resources.

Moody Publishers books help fund the training of students for ministry around the world.

The **Moody Bible Institute** is one of the most well-known Christian institutions in the world, training thousands of young people to faithfully serve Christ wherever He calls them. And when you buy and read a book from Moody Publishers, you're helping make that vital ministry training possible.

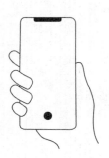

Continue to dive into the Word, *anytime, anywhere.*

Find what you need to take your next step in your walk with Christ: from uplifting music to sound preaching, our programs are designed to help you right when you need it.

Download the **Moody Radio App** and start listening today!

 MOODY Publishers®
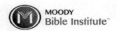 MOODY Bible Institute™
 MOODY Radio™